SUSTAINED BY FAITH
PERSONAL AWAKENING IN GOD

Dear Reader,

This wonderful book will make the very depths of your soul cry, while also giving you hope—showing you that there truly is light at the end of the tunnel of despair and pain. It is impossible to read Mary Ann Johnston's autobiography without being transformed, without seeing your life as a path with purpose.

The author is a deeply spiritual person, who bravely lived through very tough times. This book is different from other stories of people finding solace in religious convictions, as Mary Ann's faith does not come only from her Christian upbringing and beliefs. It also arises from and is continuously strengthened by blissful spiritual experiences and loving communion with Jesus and divine beings in both Christian and Hindu traditions.

Through her faith that God is always with her, helping her, the author is able to deal with difficulties in a constructive way and thus grow in soul stature.

Along the way, she finds her calling: to use her life experiences and faith to help others. This book is yet another milestone in fulfilling Mary Ann's life purpose of helping others.

Susana Stoica, PhD.
Author of *Reluctant Healer* and
Healing with the Loving Heart

Sustained by Faith

Personal Awakening in God

Mary Ann Johnston

Tatienne Publishing
Vanderbilt, Michigan

ORDERS:
http://www.sustainedbyfaith.com
http://www.TatiennePublishing.com
http://www.OutskirtsPress.com/SustainedByFaith

Johnston, Mary Ann, 1940—

Sustained by Faith – Personal Awakening in God / Mary Ann Johnston.
          1.   Religion - Spirituality
          2.   Jesus Christ—Apparitions and Miracles.
          3.   Christianity
          4.   Autobiography

Includes index.

Editor: George O. Johnston

Cover design direction & photography by Linda R. Bayer, RA, of Bayer Essence,
www.bayer-essence.com

Cover Photograph: Sun setting over Lake Michigan

Tatienne Publishing
P.O. Box 326, Vanderbilt, MI 49795

ISBN: 978-0-9817027-4-2

Library of Congress Control Number: 2008935142

Tatienne Publishing and the Tatienne Publishing logo are trademarks belonging to
Tatienne Publishing.

PRINTED IN THE UNITED STATES OF AMERICA

by Mary Ann Johnston

Sustained by Faith – Personal Awakening in God
Messages from Jesus – A Dialogue of Love

CD   Hymns of Love

Dedication

This book is dedicated to you, dear reader,

that it may kindle within you

light and love, wisdom and strength,

to sustain you and give you courage,

today and forever.

Contents

POETRY BY MARY ANN JOHNSTON

POETRY BY GEORGE JOHNSTON

Acknowledgements

Loving gratitude goes to God, Jesus, my family and friends and especially my husband, George, for his never-ending patience as my editor.

When Marilyn Beker reviewed the first draft and told me, "You need to fill in the gaps; you left a whole section of your life out. Tell me about it," I reluctantly addressed the seventeen years of abuse in my life that I wanted to forget. George unceasingly loved me throughout the ordeal and masterfully edited my writing. Truly this book is as much his as mine.

Special thanks to my daughter, Linda Bayer, who while going through her own personal trauma, gave me sound advice.

Further, thanks goes to my son, David T. Najdowski, for assisting with our website.

To all my children, who helped me remember sequences and events in our shared lives, I love you dearly.

And too, I wish to thank those who reviewed and made helpful suggestions for this book, namely, Diana Mitchell, Susan Stoica, Marilyn Beker, Dorothy Stingley, Tineke Wilders, and Millissa Probart.

Author's Note

Song of the Morning is a yoga retreat, nestled deep in the silence and beauty of a Michigan forest. My husband and I built our home in the nurturing space of a new spiritual community here. It is from this peaceful, woodland setting that I write.

Jesus started appearing to me as a friend and companion in my childhood, at a time in life when our minds are innocent and more open to Spirit. Most children lose their ability to see spirit beings or invisible friends. They realize that others can't see them, and they tend to slowly let go of the things grown-ups never saw or have long since forgotten. Or, maybe parents and peers tell them how silly they are, so they block out such subtle experiences from their awareness.

I had learned to keep secret my relationship with Jesus, as it was often frowned upon. But now, in my later years, He has urged me to write of it.

Jesus still is my "invisible friend". When He appears to me in ethereal form, I feel at one with Him and am at ease in His presence. I believe that He makes it that way, for truly, if He were to come without shielding me from His full glory, I would not be able to tolerate it. As it is, it is sometimes overwhelming.

In an effort to explain how I am able to commune with Jesus, I can only say that I have no specific technique for this and I am not sure how to explain it. Jesus is beyond space and time. I either think of Him or He just shows up, and we communicate, most often in words unspoken, in what I call "heart talk", which is superconscious, or soul, communion.

Yet, this book is not only about spiritual communion. Prior to publishing *Sustained by Faith*, I had given the manuscript to a friend to read, and she commented that there seemed to be a long period in my life that was not addressed and wanted to know what I left out. As if it were meant to be told, she drew out of me the story of my first marriage and the abuse I suffered, and then, without any hesitation, adamantly convinced me that the telling would help people. I reluctantly agreed.

It was difficult, for I found I had to force myself—out of the comfort of thirty-two years of silence—to take a step back into that time. Surprisingly, along with writing, re-writing, sharing memories with my children, and igniting new ones in them and myself, healing occurred for that which had lain dormant in us far too long, as we opened up and faced the traumas of the past. I know I have done the right thing in sharing this part of my life, for while writing about it, I was often enveloped in divine fragrances, sustaining me as I relived it.

In my openness to the spirit world, I was eventually made aware of having the gift of spiritual healing. I had been raised as a conservative Lutheran and did not have much knowledge of healers. While working as a traveling occupational therapist in hospitals, outpatient clinics and other settings, this healing ability suddenly was made known to me. I had a difficult time transitioning to my new role as a healer, for my church family did not accept the "new me" with open arms. Still this was not something I could keep secret. This was God's work and could not be set aside.

Then I had a powerful awakening, from which I became ever-more aware of Spirit. I began writing poetry describing my experiences—blissful energies flowing through me, visions of great beauty, deeper understanding, ethereal fragrances, love, oneness. This awakening separated me even more from those who don't want to hear about things they don't understand. So I came to live at the Retreat to be able to commune with God and Jesus in an accepting environment. It was here that I met my present husband, who values spiritual matters as I do.

When I started to write this book, I simply intended to share some of my spiritual experiences, for in 2002, Jesus told me I was supposed to write about them, but my manuscript grew and became an unintended autobiography.

I hope what I have experienced and learned along the way will be of value to you and that Jesus' words and the support He gave me will touch your heart. And, if this book in some way heals wounds of your own, gives you hope, feeds your meditations, ignites spiritual intuitions from deep within you, or inspires you to be more loving, it will truly have been worth its writing.

Chapter One

The Gate

Do not forget the grandmother.
Adorned in love for you,
in selfless service she came.

God saw to lay a gentle hand upon
the consequences that she faced
and gave her peace above the blame.

—*Sebastian*

Flint, Michigan, 1940 . . .

There was a papa and a thin slip of a mama with a swollen belly and a visiting family couple, gathered, one afternoon, to play cards. When suddenly, the mama laid down her cards, announced that the baby was about to be born, and they should all lay down their cards and wait for her return. Up the stairs they went, the mama, her sister-in-law and the family dog. There were four other sleeping children in the house, all under the age of six.

The doctor was summoned, but in the meantime, the baby had already made fast, quiet entry into a cold, February world, a new beginning where no starting is. But, there was no sound coming forth from the wide-awake baby, and upon arrival, the doctor carefully examined her to convince himself and the family that her silence was nothing to be concerned about.

The name "Mary Ann" had already been chosen, but it seemed an unusual choice for that family because the three older girls were called "Jo", "Jack", and "George", short for "Jolene", Jacquelyn", and "Georgia." Right from the beginning, Mary Ann didn't quite fit.

The doctor left after noting the time of birth, the date, her weight, and that she was able to suckle. And then the mama and her sister-in-law went downstairs to continue their card game. Only the family dog remained to stand guard upstairs in the darkness.

The mama was overwhelmed with all of her babies, and because of Mary Ann's quiet nature, it was easy for her to overlook and be oblivious to the child's needs. The papa simply thought all was well.

In the large city near where they lived, the papa worked and played guitar in a bar, and the mama most often went along, sitting and drinking, then coming home in the middle of the night.

Now, what happened next will be hard to believe for many of you. But, there are reasons for birth and all of life, and sometimes we come to earth with predetermined tasks. It was decided, within a council of those who know, that even though Mary Ann chose to give herself for this terrestrial mission, it was obvious that she needed more care than what the mama was capable of giving.

In timeless congress to serve Christ, the Council of Fourteen sends volunteers to earth for various tasks and oversees their progress. The Christ is the center of the lives of those who serve.

And so it was that I, Sebastian, took it upon myself to be her guardian and caregiver for as long as she needed me. Presently she needed someone in material form, and therefore, I entered the body of the gentle family dog.

In the beginning, in the stillness of the night, to arouse the mama, I would pull the blankets off her and drag them to where Mary Ann lay awake and hungry. The mama soon figured out why she was being awakened and would bring the child into the bed with her, position herself comfortably and let her suckle while she slept. It was a family joke for a while, but soon the mama took it in her stride and relied on me to wake her when the child was hungry, for the child rarely cried.

Mary Ann's needs had to be in line with the needs of four other children, and soon another baby followed. Suckling was no longer an option for Mary Ann, and milk was scarce. Still, Mary Ann rarely cried.

Grandparents often came to visit, bringing with them what food and comforts they could afford. The Great

Depression was barely ending, and there was still little to be had.

When Mary Ann was about one year of age, just learning to walk, I, Sebastian, sensing danger before it happened, jumped up just in time to get between her and the hot wood stove she was falling onto. The burns I received were nothing compared to what might have been for the child.

Mary Ann, feeling sadness, cared for my wounds and comforted me the best way she could. She would curl up with me near the wood stove in sweet, loving companionship, stroking me back to health with her intrinsic healing ability.

She often spent her nights with me, rather than with her siblings. Even on summer nights we sought each other out. Love brings a different way of being in the world.

Her parents were not aware of the fact that a puff of wind would blow her over. She needed more help than what I, Sebastian, could offer. It was time to move on.

In urgent heart song, I sang her needs to the council. Soon thereafter, on her second birthday, her grandparents came to visit. I would like to say it was I, but it was Mary Ann herself who instilled in her grandmother her needs, through the language of love within an embrace, and the grandmother became wholly aware of Mary Ann's lean body. And the grandmother knew what she had to do. . . .

Oh, Grandmother,
of ancient holiness,
who opened up to
where love is set—
where sound
and silence embrace—
you felt her grace.

And here in this remembrance,
sprung to life
so lately born,
you saw
the reflection of God's will
and let it be your own.

Secretly, the grandmother began making small hand-sewn articles of clothing: simple dresses, under-things, nightgowns, a lavender snowsuit so beautiful that many years later it was talked of. Designed as if a riding suit, it flared out at the hips and buttoned tight at the ankles. A jaunty bonnet was with it.

The loving grandmother matched the silence of the child, telling no one what she was up to. As she finished each article, she would fold it and lay it lovingly in a bag. The grandfather could only stand by and wonder while the bag became full.

One day in April of 1942, when they were preparing to make a visit to the grandmother's sister some distance away, the grandmother announced to the grandfather that she wanted to pick Mary Ann up and take her along for the weekend. The time was right, secret letters had been sent, waiting had to end. The filled bag, together with a lunch, was placed in the car.

There was no reason for her parents to be concerned. And so the family easily consented, since the absence of one child among many would hardly be noticed for such a requested short absence.

Adorned in blessings, Mary Ann took hold of her loving grandmother's hand, and I, Sebastian, knowing all, left the body of the family dog and followed in spirit.

I watched Mary Ann with pleasure as they drove through the countryside. She went from one side of the back seat to the other . . . looking . . . looking out the windows. The trip into the country opened up a new world for her, revealing so much to behold that, finally overcome with the immensity of the adventure, she lay down in the back seat of the car and slept.

Upon arrival at the grandmother's family farm, Mary Ann got out of the car, looked up and became lost in the vastness of the deep blue sky. With head tilted back, she fell backward onto the ground. She lay there, looking deep into the sky, comfortably lost in time, until her grandfather came along and scooped her up, as easily as if he were picking up a shoe.

Just over two years of age, Mary Ann was a scrawny child, with limbs seemingly longer than they needed to be for want of baby fat. She kept close to her grandmother and grandfather, the only familiar faces she knew. The child looked about in wonder, for she had never been on a farm before. So much was new for her—new surroundings, new people, and unfamiliar animals.

No one seemed to realize the significance of these new experiences. No one gave it a thought that Mary Ann had never seen a cow or a chicken or an expanse of countryside, nor so many trees and sky and space.

Soon after arriving, there was one woman, Emmy, who paid special attention to Mary Ann, more so than anyone else. She brought a ball with her and played with the child.

Emmy was unable to have children and had desperately wanted a child. For Emmy, the waiting was over, for the grandmother had sent letters ahead, planning in secret to give Mary Ann to her. Emmy also brought with her an orange, a true gift in those long-ago days. She peeled it and fed Mary Ann a section, and she devoured it, wanting more and more. Juice ran down her face and she couldn't seem to get enough for her hungry body. Finally she was satisfied, only to abruptly throw it all up, for her malnourished condition was such that she could not tolerate an abundance of food so fast.

Emmy cleaned Mary Ann up, gently bathing her face and hands with a soft, warm, wet cloth. Then with nary a glance back, Mary Ann willingly, in all innocence, climbed into this woman's car and, with barely a farewell, she left her loving grandparents and her old life behind, with no mind as to where she was going or why. With only dances of sweetness within her mind, she once again fell asleep on her way to a new home, a new family, and a new life.

Chapter Two

Innocence

THE OWL AND THE FLOWER

A little flower stood by the wayside.
Along came a wise old owl.
The owl said to the flower:
"How do you do it? You look so innocent and pure.
Did you study Plato or practice austerities
to become what you are?
Did you go to finishing school
to discover how to be beautiful?"

Amazed, the little flower said:
"I don't know. I guess I just grew up
the way I was supposed to."
The little flower smiled,
and the owl shook his ruffled head.
"Sure beats me," he said.

—George Johnston

I have no memory of those first twenty-seven months of my life. It is only through conversations with my grandmother—who, years later, undeservedly, felt she needed to beg my forgiveness for giving me away—an aunt, a sister and my foster mother, along with what Sebastian has instilled in me, that I learned of my uncommon beginnings.

When my foster mother, Emmy, brought me home, I met her husband, Ray. I soon began to call them Mom and Dad. Mom wore the pants in the family in a firm but fair way. My father had a gentle nature about him and he abided by her rule. He was a good man. I loved them both.

According to my foster mom, my body filled out quickly from three healthy meals each day. I finally had baby fat.

She told me I did not appear to miss my birth family at all. I never asked for my parents, grandparents, siblings or even the family dog, seemingly nonattached. Nor did I appear to feel remorse because of being given away.

I am grateful for my birth family and have always felt that I was born to my birth parents so that I would in turn be given to my foster parents, who couldn't have children, thus ending up where I was supposed to be.

Sometime after I came to live with them, a friendly dog would come to the house and sit by the door until I came outside. Just as it must have been with the family dog in my infancy, we communicated with heart talk and my childish chatter, as if we were old friends. I would take a hairbrush and brush him down the best I could while singing impromptu melodies to him. And I would think nothing of it to wipe away his drool with my hands and wipe it on my clothing.

I have a picture of him and me, when I was about four years old—my coat unbuttoned and a floppy hat on my head in comic disarray, standing by him. We were so happy. My foster parents never found out where he lived.

We went to church on Sundays, where Dad sang in the choir. We didn't have pictures of Jesus in our home and rarely talked about Jesus during the week; no dinner prayers or night-time prayers. The only representation of Jesus I was familiar with was a cross in our church with Jesus on it, and I was uncomfortable with that. It was a scary thing.

One of my earliest memories is of an event that had a major impact on the rest of my life. I was five years old and excited to finally be old enough to attend Sunday School. It was my very-first day and I vividly recall the teacher showing us a full-length picture of Jesus. I remember how joyous and relieved I was to see Jesus alive and well and not on a cross.

In the picture He had blue eyes. He wore an ankle length, flowing robe, with a mantle thrown over His shoulder, both slightly off-white in color. His beard was average in length and full, not pointed. His wavy hair, brown and parted in the middle, was just past shoulder length. He appeared slender, tall. But to a very small child everyone was tall. He emanated a sense of strength. I remember His hands were big, with long, pointed fingers. His feet were bare, except for sandals.

The Sunday school teacher said, "Jesus is your friend. He is with you all the time. You can talk to Him, and He will hear you and talk to you." At that, He suddenly, simply came out of that picture as if He had come alive. I remember His gaze . . . His sparkling, fiery eyes were looking deep within me, as if He was searching for something. He shined, as if He were a lamp.

Suddenly, I felt like I was in a short tunnel facing Him. Everything else was obscured by fog . . . dream-like. I felt myself going to Him as He was coming to me, and yet I had not taken a step. I felt no fear, just happiness, in His presence.

As I relive that moment in time, I feel the same whole-body wave of warmth flowing through me, causing me to smile.

I don't remember anything more than that. But ever since that day, Jesus has been only a breath away and, to this day, has never changed His appearance to me.

It is not with physical senses that I experience Jesus' presence. He appears in a manner that transcends ordinary explanation. There is no doubt in my mind that it is Jesus who comes to me, for when He does, His loving essence filters into my very being.

It seemed as natural to see Jesus and talk with Him as with anyone else. There was nothing hidden between us. I loved His sweet presence. He would appear to me in ethereal form, and at times would wrap me in His mantle or I would lean into Him, and I felt as if I were sinking into a shimmer of His being, into a oneness with Him that I had no words for as a child and even now can barely explain. I went about my childhood simply knowing He was there for me, and I am sure I took Him for granted, just as one takes one's parents for granted.

It was a surprise to me when I realized others did not really see or hear Him. People sang songs in church about the nearness of Jesus, such as *In the Garden*, which has the words, "He walks with me and He talks with me. . . ."

I wondered how they could sing hymns that depict Jesus as a living, personal friend and comforter, and yet not accept the reality of it. When I would try to point this out to my pastor and Sunday School teacher, I could feel their energy change and saw a shadow about them as they tuned me out—something adults often do with children.

I soon learned to keep my beautiful friendship with Jesus a big secret. It was like having an invisible friend; if you talk about it people make fun of you. Children usually give up their invisible friends before long because of pressure from others, but my love for Jesus kept me from losing Him.

I often wished I could speak with those people who wrote about Jesus in their hymns, for surely they knew Him like I knew Him. Just the thought that they were like me gave me comfort and made me feel less alone.

As this small child, I wondered where Jesus went when I

wasn't aware of His presence or where He lived at night while I slept. One day in church after a service, I bravely walked up to the altar to get a good look at Jesus on the cross to see if He looked the same as when He appeared to me. I was confused, for He truly did not look like the Jesus I had come to know.

I turned away. To the left was the pastor's study, and the pastor was standing in the doorway. I walked over to him. I must have been very small, because I remember looking way up at him. I didn't enter the room; I just stood at the doorway, pointed into the room behind him, and asked, "Is this where Jesus lives?" He looked startled at first and then said, "Yes." So now I knew where Jesus lived: in the pastor's study.

I have many sweet memories of doing things with Jesus as a child. To others, it might have seemed like I was a loner. My mother once said to me, "You liked your own company." She never truly understood that Jesus was keeping me company, even though I talked to her of it.

We had fun together, Jesus and I. We would go fishing on the pier in Manistee, and Jesus would tell me where to cast my line. Others might not be catching much, but I always caught a lot of perch. When Jesus would tell me to put two hooks on my line, I would catch two perch at a time. So it was very handy to have Jesus as my friend.

We would sit on a railing, at the corner of Sibben and First Street in my neighborhood, and wave to everyone driving by. If only they realized who was with me, waving at them!

My father wanted me to have piano lessons, and he found out that the school was offering group lessons for fifty cents. They were to be held at the Manistee Recreation Association building. So he gave me the fifty cents, and after school I was to go there for the lesson.

I went to the building and couldn't open the big, unwelcoming side doors. I was about seven years old then. Since I couldn't get in, I went to the store and bought candy. The next week my father gave me another fifty cents, and instead of going to the intimidating building, I went straight to the store for candy. I had no concept of guilt.

Then he asked me, "So, show me what you have learned." I sat at the piano and played "music" that only a child would understand. He said nothing; no blame, no questions. This might have been a good opportunity for my parents to teach me a lesson and make me feel guilty but they didn't.

The next Saturday my father took me by the hand, and we walked four blocks to a welcoming house, where lived a piano teacher, who taught me how to play the piano, and fed me cookies, and tea from delicate cups, after every lesson. Many years later, when the piano teacher passed on, my mother went to her estate sale and bought the lovely tea china for me.

I made my singing debut at the age of seven also. I went to the radio station and sang on "Aunt Nanny's" radio show. The first song I ever sang in public was "We Are

Climbing Jacob's Ladder." I was asked back often. I even played the piano one time on the radio program. I lost my place in the music and started over from the beginning, taking up most of the rest of the program. I remember seeing someone behind a glass window in the studio, looking frantic as I played on and on. I was never asked to play piano on that program again. I had no sense of time restraints. It makes me laugh when I think of it.

I continued to experience, from time to time, the same blissful energies that rose and spread within me when I first encountered Jesus in Sunday school. Sometimes this happened for no apparent reason or when I felt close to God, or I would will it to happen while concentrating on my breathing. Often it happened when Jesus was with me, for His uplifting presence was very powerful. The energy rising within me happened often enough that I took it for granted, and I would probably never mention it except that I now realize it was not the norm.

Back then, if you had asked me, I would have described the energy I felt, as warm fuzzies filling me up, a sweet spread of energy, from my feet to the top of my head, somewhat like the feeling some people get when they are thrilled by a newborn baby or beautiful music. I loved the feeling. The energy always brought on an instant smile and sometimes laughter. Occasionally I would fall over. Early on, I would direct the energy to certain areas of my body, or slow my breathing down to quiet myself into no thought. I loved the stillness beyond thought. It was far more peaceful than even the peaceful life I lived. My mother knew that something was different, as she would sometimes find me in a quiet state. Later she would question what I was doing. I didn't know how to answer her. She recently said, "You were often in your own world, but I never felt a need to have you checked over by a doctor!"

I was walking home from school one day, alone. I was seven years old. I remember suddenly stepping up onto a cement step leading to someone's house. I stood on that lone step and emphatically announced out loud to no one in particular, "I want to be alive to see the end of the world!" I have no idea where that declaration came from. There was nothing to prompt it. Nor had I ever thought about the future. The thought of the world ending was so profound to me that I have never forgotten it.

When I was about eight or nine years old, I would write sermons and make some of my friends sit and listen to me. I am not sure they appreciated it. I wish I had those sermons today. It would be interesting to read what I wrote back then.

In those growing-up years, I was instilled with the desire to serve God. I would tell my friends I wanted to be a missionary, and they accepted that. It didn't feel as if Jesus was guiding me toward any specific vocation, but I knew of no other way I could serve God.

As a senior in high school, it was mandatory to see the class counselor when you were nearing graduation. I went to see her, and she asked me, "What do you want to do with your life?" I said, "I want to go to Columbus University and become a missionary." And in one fell-swoop, she dashed my hopes, adamantly saying, "Don't be silly. Your family can't afford to send you to college and to be a missionary as a woman is impractical." As if she had the final say in my future, I accepted that, but was confused by what I considered the loss of my life's purpose. I had never been counseled by my parents or through school or church about obtaining scholarships for college or offered help in pursuing a career, so these options seemed out of reach.

Taking my sorrow to Jesus during that time, He instilled in me,

"You can serve God in all aspects of your life by simply doing everything with love."

My parents were of the mind-set that, after graduation, one should be on their own as soon as possible. Living at home was not an option, my job did not pay enough for me to live on my own, and college was not an option either. Marriage seemed to be my only choice.

Thus, at the age of nineteen—a year after graduating from high school—I married, as if this were the thing to do.

Chapter Three

Sticks and Stones

For Thou art with me;
Thy rod and Thy staff,
they comfort me.
— Psalms 23: 4

Findings and statistics are indented and interspersed
throughout this chapter. References can be found in
the End Notes at the back of the book. Keep in mind
that victims can be men and children, as well as
women.

I am convinced that my first husband, Dave, and I didn't
understand how love must be continually expressed by both
partners in a marriage in order for it to succeed. There
should be classes in high school like Leo Buscaglia's[1]
college course, "Love 101." I think college is too late.

I didn't really know what abuse was. It had no name for me and no form. It was never mentioned and I never saw it at home with my parents. If you had asked me what abuse was back then, I might have said it was someone physically hurting someone else. I never dreamed it could be more than that. We didn't have a television set until I was in my teens, and in those days, abuse was rarely shown on TV. We watched shows like *Red Skelton*. At first, I wouldn't watch it, thinking it had something to do with a skeleton.

In our early "going-together," high school times, Dave was very possessive and controlling. He was jealous of my male classmates and would become angry when I simply acknowledged them on the street while with him, although he was friendly with other girls.

This jealousy was a bit flattering at first, but became offensive very quickly and it made me angry. Whenever I stood up for myself, he would try to make me feel I was in the wrong. I could never convince him that the occasional greetings to other males were innocent.

I was concerned about the myriad of feelings I was experiencing, especially the anger. In an early-morning communion with Jesus, I asked Him how I might control my anger. He made clear that

"No one can make you angry except yourself."

A common threat from Dave was, "If you don't do (or stop) this you must not love me, so I will commit suicide."

A very controlling statement. It brought fear into my life. Fear that he would do such a thing.

"The threat is truly to his very being, for more than the body is the soul. His choice; not yours.

"Do not tarry upon the fear, for it is his fear. It is not your path."

I wrote a letter to his brother, Father John, a Catholic priest. It was never acknowledged, nor do I know if he ever talked to Dave about his suicide threats.

Once, when I tried to save a kitten from being tormented by him, he put his hands around my neck, supposedly all in fun, but choked me until I began to pass out.

Such events happened infrequently, interspersed with puppy love, so I dismissed them without serious thought. Were they a precursor of more abuse to come? Statistics indicate they were.

> **In one study, from 20-30 percent of female high school students reported having already experienced teen dating violence.[2]**

I was entering a dark trial of my life, like a lamb at the very feet of humanity's lowest ebb. And Jesus was letting me use my free will[3] to make my own choices.

Dave became a self-employed, mason contractor after dissolving a partnership with his brother in a construction business. I worked in a library. We had never sat down to go over a budget or even considered how we would support a family down the road. There were no plans for our future.

Dave always had a problem with drinking, and I never knew what to expect from him. He most often came home when the bars closed and spent less and less time with me.

> Living with abuse numbs the victim so that they may be unable to recognize that they are involved in a set pattern of abuse.[4]

Once, while in a drunken, belligerent state, he humiliated me in front of a birth-sister, who was visiting from out of state. She didn't come back to see me again for thirty-five years.

What had I gotten myself into? I was pregnant, and I felt I couldn't possibly back out of our marriage. He was unpredictable, but always sweet after misbehaving or losing control of his temper. Our relationship was like a caress, followed by a slap, followed by a caress. Even though Jesus was near and dear to me, I was still receiving remorseless trials from Dave. It was like a dichotomy of agony and ecstasy.

> Often, the abuser is quite loving and lovable when they are not being abusive.[5]

Sometimes, I had dreams so beautiful that I thought God must have initiated them. Prayer dreams, like songs in the night, conversing with God. And often upon waking, Jesus would speak to me about life's experiences, good and bad, and how they have a purpose, which often is to build one's moral strength, to learn to care for oneself, and to relate to others.

He gave me dignity, not through praise but through heartfelt love, as if I truly mattered, and instilled in me the thought, *"Be strong."*

On a December afternoon in 1960, our daughter Linda was born with relative ease. She was beautiful. I thought Dave would change now that he had a child.

Bills were coming in that he should have taken care of when he was paid for completing a construction job. He told me not to worry about it but the bills kept piling up. Winter set in and construction jobs stopped. He had no intention of looking for other work. We moved in with his mother for the winter, and I went back to work.

When I suggested that we go on welfare, he was infuriated. He considered it beneath him. We had a final discussion about this in the car, and as he drove down the road, he backhanded me . . . blood ran down my face; my surroundings faded. I came to; realizing the sacredness of my marriage was no more.

> Approximately three million women are physically abused by their husband or boyfriend per year. [6]

> When a partner constantly refuses to listen to your feelings, that is, unquestionably, mental abuse. [7]

I often struggled with trying to see the presence of God in abuse and trying to understand how someone could be abusive in the presence of God. If we truly knew how our negative behaviors defiled God's sacred space, we would never abuse another soul, never say an unkind word or think an unkind thought.

Sometimes, Jesus would remind me of the presence of God when I was sorely challenged. He would begin by saying, *"My words are only for those who will hear,"* and then I would listen.

A few times, He said, *"God is your strength!"* Another time, He said, *"Love endures all things."*

And too, blissful energy would often fill me, erasing negative thoughts, and sustain me.

Although some of Dave's family were very church oriented, he did not share my desire to go to church. He didn't understand my relationship with Jesus and thought of it as something abnormal. His indifference didn't really matter, as I was content to keep this sacred part of my life to myself.

In the spring, we moved back to the cottage. A friend I worked with at the library invited me to her wedding. Several of the other employees decided to go together. I had to ask Dave for permission to go. He reluctantly gave his consent.

I had a great time dancing. I had not had such a fun time in quite a while and I loved to dance. I arrived home just after midnight and was met at the door by Dave carrying our baby daughter. He started to scream obscenities at me and knocked me to the floor, then he kicked me from top to bottom while shouting degrading assumptions at me and telling me I was "no good, nothing" and nothing was mine including Linda.

The abuser lashes out with violent behavior as a power play designed to show the victim "who is boss."[8]

As he kicked me, Jesus' face appeared in front of Dave's, and I instantly willed myself out of my body. While being held in a light that calmed me, I suddenly was not feeling, but somehow indirectly knowing, how it felt. I saw Dave kicking me, over and over, and I could only think that Linda should not have to witness this.

And somehow, in some way, I felt sadness for Dave.

Studies suggest that between 3.3 and 10 million children are exposed to domestic violence annually.[9]

I wanted out right then and there, for this was not the first time, and the feeling never left me. I questioned Jesus, "Why is this happening to me?" The thought came to me that experience precedes growth. I didn't want to hear that. From my perspective, it seemed a harsh thought that couldn't have come from Jesus.

When I was finally brave enough to tell my husband I wanted a divorce, he flew into a rage with uncontrolled ranting, "How could you possibly bring shame to Father John (his brother, a Catholic priest). If we were divorced it would ruin him as a priest." He raised his fists and came down on the top of my head, and I crumbled to the floor. I lay there, unconscious, and when I came to, he showed no concern about me. I felt like I died inside.

Later, I asked myself, "How could he possibly think that drunkenness and rage could be excused but not divorce?"

There may be religious and extended family pressure to keep the family together no matter what.[10]

Through heart talk, in wordless expression colored by shades of hopelessness, I implored Jesus, "If all is one in God, how could such darkness be light?" The only answer that emanated from Jesus was *"love."* I felt His love flow through my whole being, and I was being made aware that Jesus had more concern for my eternal life as a whole than my misery of the moment.

Domestic abuse happens more often than car accidents, mugging, and rape combined.[11]

In 1961, near the family cottage, there were forty acres for sale, with a house, small barn, and a garage, for $10,000 on a land contract with a low down payment. Dave had to have it. Surely it would have been wonderful to have. I too wanted a home, but we had not had to pay rent up to then and I couldn't see how we could afford it, plus I wasn't even sure I would remain with him.

Discussing it rationally was not an option. He would not reason it out with me. He had not listened to me before and had no intention of starting now. He asked his mother for the down payment and we moved into our own home.

Initially we were happy in our new home. Dave was even nicer to me for a time. He promised me he would pay his construction bills when they came in and pay his mother back, but this was short-lived. Dave wouldn't consider steady work of any kind. Yet he always had money to spend on drinks and bought horses and mules and farm equipment, though he had no intention of farming. My income did not cover all the bills. And he had a new threat, "Everything is mine."

Sometimes when Jesus would come to me without being called upon, I knew it meant something significant was about to happen. At that time of my life it was more likely to be trauma.

One day, while playing on the floor with Linda, a simple thought of Jesus filled me with beautiful, sweet energy. Time instantly slowed down. I looked at Linda to determine if she was experiencing the same thing, and she was playing with her toys as if nothing was happening. Yet she turned to me a few times with a beautiful smile upon her face, while brilliant light touched everything. I so wanted her to be fully aware of this moment. I felt joy seeing Linda so enveloped in light.

Fragrance filled the air, and I sat back to take it in, trying desperately to get as much of it as I could before it would take its leave, for I knew it would. With each deep breath, the energy built within until it was all that I could tolerate. My preoccupation with survival faded as I was momentarily lifted into ecstasy. Then, suddenly, fragrant bliss stayed my breath. I felt I could have held my breath forever without effort.

Oh, how I longed to remain in that bliss forever! How

can I express this in words? Words are inadequate. What peace, what joy, what brilliance! No abuse, no mar anywhere, no spot, no ugliness.

The next day, I caught Dave having sex with a very young neighbor girl in our barn. She might have been fourteen. He blatantly flaunted his manhood in front of me. I was stunned and numb.

> Emotional abuse can take the form of: provocative behavior with the opposite sex, humiliation, and control.[12]

I became pregnant again. Sex with Dave had become disgusting for me when I realized he was having sex with others. I could only succumb. I was afraid of his strength, afraid to fight back. I was unable to give him what he needed. I felt raped.

My pregnancy was difficult. I don't even remember where Dave was most of the time. He was not present for me.

> Most research reports that abuse against women escalates during pregnancy. One study found that 37 percent of obstetric patients were physically abused during pregnancy.[13]

In November, 1961, our beautiful son, John, our beloved Father John's namesake, died of hyaline membrane (lung disorder) when one day old, after a long labor and Caesarean birth. I had John near my heart for nine months and never got to hold him after his birth. No one else was as close to him as I. Dave and his family, without telling me anything or asking about my thoughts, had a quick funeral while I was still in the hospital.

I would turn to Jesus for comfort. It was like Jesus was in my life to sustain me. I would hold Him in my thoughts and breathe in and be filled with blissful energy, as if this were cleansing and strengthening me within.

Often when I prayed, I just knew He was near. He wasn't always visible, but I knew in my heart He was with me, like my shadow.

I had changed my religion from the Lutheran to the Catholic faith to marry Dave, even though he rarely went to church. I knew my relationship with God and Jesus was not going to change just because I went to a different church. I would have been comfortable in a mosque, temple or cave. To me, religions are man-made approximations of truth, embedded with tradition and dogma, all worshipping the same God.

One winter morning, in the still of darkness as I lay sleeping, Dave came into the bedroom all in a rush and shouted, "The house is on fire. You need to get out of the house!" I thought I was having a nightmare. Dave kept shouting at me. Then I realized I was not dreaming. I jumped up, put on my slippers and bathrobe, woke Linda and wrapped her up in blankets, and rushed into the kitchen shouting, "Did you call the fire department?" He said, "No, leave . . . the ceiling is on fire in the basement and the floor is ready to cave in!" I raced from the house, took the car to go get help, and in my confusion got stuck in the deep snow in our yard. I had to get out of the car and carry Linda in the snowstorm to the neighbors to get help. Their phone lines were down because of the weather. By the time help was summoned, the house was gone. We lost everything.

Later, when the neighbor's phone was working, I was sitting on a stairway in their house talking to my grandmother on the phone while holding Linda on my lap. Suddenly I was overwhelmed by the presence of Jesus. I was pregnant again, and clutching my stomach as though to protect the life within me, I rocked the three of us and cried my heart out. The women gathered there took Linda and let me cry, not realizing that it was Jesus Himself who prompted this needed release.

I moved as if in a trance, for weeks. It was not a sea of bliss, just a sea. I was unmotivated and simply followed orders and did what I had to do. We moved in with his mother once again. I worked and did my job.

I would get up in the morning, put one foot before the other, bathe, dress, take care of Linda, deliver her to a babysitter so Dave would be free to do his "nothing" during the wintry days, and go to work. The next day and every day after that, I would do the same thing.

When the weather improved, we moved from Dave's mother's back into the family cottage. Soon after, a neighbor came over and asked if we would like to buy their home, since they were moving. I sadly, simply lifted my empty hands in the air. There was no money that I knew of.

I floated along in life. That is the best description I can think of . . . floating. It seemed as if my life was to be one of servitude . . . to my husband, with no questions asked. He often took his frustrations out on me in emotional and physical abuse, hitting me where it would not show. How could I possibly serve God in this situation? I was stuck.

> Domestic abuse is about batterers using their control, not always losing their control. Their actions are very deliberate.[14]

I started having sleeping problems and anxiety attacks. My bodily functions were messed up. My self-esteem had hit bottom. I tried to turn myself outside in, into my center of being, to the point of disappearing. I simply wanted to go to God forever.

My doctor's answer was to put me on strong tranquilizers, even though I was pregnant again.

A priest I went to talk to told me I should be a "martyr" for the sake of the children.

This old priest emphatically implied that, as a woman, I had duties to fullfill, and I should succumb to the will of my husband, bow low and endure! He also implied that I didn't count, and the incidents of abuse must have been my fault! I got the impression that he thought the word "martyr" would make me feel special. But how does succumbing to the will of an abusive husband make one feel special?!

While he talked, I felt such a demeaning attitude toward me coming out of this old priest. At first I felt sorry for him and thought to myself, "You poor thing!", for I saw a darkness clinging to him. Then, as if cold water had been thrown in my face, I felt intense anger at the priest, my husband, and so many others I knew who displayed the same controlling paternalism toward the women in their lives.

Overwhelmed by the feelings I was freeing—which had lain dormant all my married life—I saw this old priest as no better than my husband! Infuriated with him and no longer listening, I left his office in a rush, in between his relentless words.

Never have I been treated this way in my relationship with Jesus. Never has Jesus looked upon me as less than or better than a man—only as a soul—seeing each of us as equal and divine in essence. In the Bible, Paul said that there is no male or female for we are all one in Christ.[15]

And now, suddenly, in all His glory, Jesus rushes into my heart—as if at one with my reliving—revealing words that feel angry and foreign to me.

"Oh, you mortals! Men and women are see-through mirrors unto themselves!"

And I envisioned a man and a woman looking into a mirror, looking beyond the superficial reflection of their physical image to see their real nature as spirit, which is neither male nor female. Then Jesus said . . .

"Look deep—beware—for those who have falsely portrayed God have not yet learned!"

And a thought came to me, as if I drew it in with my breath. I knew He meant those who act as though God would judge one gender as better than the other have not yet learned.

There was more, but I couldn't write of it. I wept, and I felt like I was weeping for all humankind.

I didn't know what to do about my life and my children's future. Standing up to my husband was out of the question. It was downright dangerous.

At this point in my life, my conversations with Jesus were more about keeping me from becoming hardened and keeping my soul intact. Many times throughout my life He has instilled in me, *"More than the body is the soul."*

One evening, as I sat at home and my husband was out, some neighbors came to visit. They were very poor, with a whole houseful of children. But they seemed happy. Dean said, "You don't have any food in your house. Have you eaten?"

What could I say? I finally told them that I had fed Linda but didn't have any food for myself. I immediately realized I was putting myself in jeopardy of a beating by saying anything to anyone. Still, I didn't say what I would have liked to say, which was, "Dave would not lower himself to put his family on welfare, but I could go hungry while he sat in a bar, and that was okay." His family and mine would have given us food if we had asked, but he would not allow me to ask.

> Abusers protect themselves from shame and
> humiliation in front of the community, through
> controlling threats.[16]

The neighbors took Linda and me home with them, and
on the way we drove past our burned-out house. Down in
the yard were Dave's car and another car that I recognized
as belonging to someone I suspected he was having a
relationship with. Oh, how my heart sank further than I
thought possible! It was like hitting me when I was already
down.

In 1963, we had another beautiful daughter, Lorelei, my
second Caesarean birth. Dave's idea of being with me in
the hospital was a hello and goodbye, ending with a
glimpse of the baby. He never stayed around for doctors'
opinions or to see to my needs. I was not his priority.

I bravely left Dave when Lorelei was a toddler. I took an
apartment in town for the girls and me, worked at the
library, and went on assistance. Still, it wasn't long before
he showed up and convinced me to go back to him, with
the promise of taking us out of town this time, away from
his buddies and women, and getting a really good job . . . a
fresh start.

Why would I go back to him? For the sake of the
children? What did this relationship ever offer that was
rewarding? Did I really consider what it would take to
make it safe enough to go back? Did I really believe that,
with a change in environment, the abuse would stop? It
seemed, if he was willing to leave town, a big sacrifice on

his part, the least I could do was try once again. I prayed I was doing the right thing in going back. I felt intuitively as if Jesus approved of our trying to keep our family together.

More than half of battered women stay with their batterer because they see a chance for improvement.[17]

We packed up, put all our belongings on a small trailer, and headed for Saginaw, Michigan. We stayed with relatives and Dave got a good job. We soon had an apartment and everything felt promising. I had a husband and the children had their father. But this was short lived: It wasn't long before he made new friends and started going into the bars again. And the abuse started up again.

In 1968, a few weeks before our son, David, was born, we bought a house-trailer, had it moved onto a piece of property near Vassar, Michigan, set it on blocks, and moved in.

While I was in the hospital and then recuperating at home, Dave's mother came to help. When she left, he still had not dug a trench to run a water pipe from the pump to the trailer. That meant there was no water in the house.

Once again there was agony and ecstasy . . . as if to prove that ordinary human life is made up of contrasting opposites, or dualities. To have something we could call home and a new son was exciting for me, and yet the agony was there in the effort it took to make it a sound home. Having a roof to call our own did not make for a happy home.

Just out of the hospital, after having had a third caesarean surgery, I had to go out to the pump to fill pails with water and bring them into the house. Pail by pail, I took water in to fill the bathtub and containers for cooking and drinking, and to flush toilets. Then, because Dave wasn't doing it, I also took it upon myself to start digging the trench to run the water line from the pump to the trailer. Dave came home, looked into the trench, and told me I had dug it too narrow and I would have to finish it! My heart sank. How could he be so thoughtless. After I finished the digging, he had someone put in the piping.

He never closed in the bottom of the trailer, so the pipes would freeze every winter, we never had working electricity on one half of the trailer, which was a double-wide, and we never had steps out the front door. I drew plans for adding on to the trailer; something Dave was capable of building. We lived there eight years, but it never happened.

Once I waited for over a week for him to dig up the drain pipes under the trailer, which he determined to be the solution for a plugged up drain. I finally decided to do it myself. A neighbor saw me doing it and reprimanded Dave for allowing me to do such work. Dave felt humiliated and beat me for that.

He was careful not to hurt me physically in front of the children, but he thought nothing of doing it late at night when he would come home drunk or at other times behind closed doors with sounds emanating through the thin walls.

Our daughter, Linda, recently said to me, "On occasion I would sit up in the corner of my bed crying as I heard him hurting you." Lorelei said the same and added she was afraid.

Not all spouse batterers are physically abusive to their children. However, all children living in a home with domestic violence experience emotional and psychological abuse when one parent is violent towards the other.[18]

We went to Father John's church, for Lorelei to make her first communion. Not ever having tasted wine or been warned that it might taste sour, she made a face when she sipped it. Father John reprimanded her in front of everyone. When she came to sit with us, Dave held her in a pinch for the rest of the mass. At the end of the service, he would not let her get in line with the other children to be congratulated, but made us all go out into the car to leave.

Father John rushed over to the car and begged Dave to let us all stay for a dinner prepared for us. At the dinner table, feeling Lorelei's distress, I began to uncontrollably sob and finally had to excuse myself. All this because a little girl made a face while sipping wine for the first time.

Chapter Four

Grass In Winter

Tears gather in my eyes
from the reliving.
Sorrow clings to my heart.

Jesus is my strength:
Surely I will endure
'till I am strong again.

The children and I took as much enjoyment out of life as we could. Life in the trailer was not all bad. There was much for the children to do outside. And indoors we had an art drawer in the kitchen, and I would save envelopes from our mail, for the envelope made a nice sheet of paper when fully opened, worthy of drawing, coloring or painting upon. I allowed the children to freely use scissors, and we made glue with flour and water. We had findings from magazines, catalogs and whatever else we could gather for artwork. Later on, two of my children went to art schools.

In the morning when I woke them with "Rise and shine," I meant it. We grew seeds in pots. We made snickerdoodles, for they were the cheapest cookies you could make. We took walks and gathered wild flowers for bouquets. We sang together. The children played in a wonderful sand-hill behind the trailer. They never sat in front of a television except for morning cartoons. I fed them at the table, three meals a day, for that was how I was raised. They played with our dog, Rusty. He was like one of them. I am sure he either understood English or could read our minds.

Rusty was a mix of shepherd and husky. He was a large dog, and many people were afraid of him. We were having a yard sale one weekend. Out of a car came two women and a bunch of children. When it came time to leave, the women, using foul language, ordered the children to come to the car. At this, Rusty ferociously woofed once, as if to say, "Be nice." The women didn't see it that way and quickly got into their car, and waited until the children were ready to leave.

Occasionally, we would haul a utility trailer from Vassar to Manistee to see family, with Rusty tied in the trailer. He would get as excited as the children when we were getting close to their grandma and grandpa's house.

He would stand in line with the children and take his turn to run and sit his bottom down, to slide on ice in the winter.

I often saw Rusty sitting and looking about. He would

sit for long periods of time. I wondered what he saw in just sitting, and one day I put the children down for naps and joined him. I sat alongside of him, as I did so often as a child with the Labrador.

I credit Rusty for teaching me to meditate on nature and to see things as they really are, for greater awareness of movement and growth in our immediate environment, for seeing the trees sway invitingly, for my being more aware of the sacred sparks in the sky. When I think of him, I think of how I loved him and he loved us. He was our friend.

Everyone thought Rusty was their dog. He was. He was everyone's for this reason or that. He was my dog too. He was an outdoor dog. He was there when I would sleepwalk outdoors. He would walk at my side until I woke—startled, but comforted by his presence.

On three occasions, when we were outside, he started to bark and growl at us for no apparent reason, scaring us so that I gathered the children and ran inside. Once inside, we would look out the window to see if we could determine what was going on with him, and out of the woods a pack of dogs would come running. He did the same thing, one day, when the children came home on the school bus. He would not let them off the bus. So the bus driver had to drive right up to the door. A pack of dogs showed up just as the children were coming in.

He was an outdoor dog and would sleep by our back entrance door at night. Eventually he had cancer, and we knew we had to have him put down. Sadly and reluctantly, we decided on the day. The night before, he whined at the door. This was not like him at all. We brought him inside, and taking his time, he went around to each of us. And each of us in turn gave him our love. We tried to feed him and he wouldn't take anything. Then he went to the door and wanted out. We never saw him again. He went away to die, sparing us the ordeal of having him put to sleep.

One day, Dave asked me who had come over, for he didn't recognize the tire tracks on the driveway, which he kept careful watch over. I told him a certain neighbor lady had been to visit, and he immediately got in his car and went to ask her if she had been over. He always accused me of having affairs while he was at work!

There were good times too. We would go on long drives together, with the children. Dave loved to two-track through the woods, always with a six-pack of beer. We found a store that had wonderful bratwurst and homemade bread, and we sometimes found our way there through the back-country roads.

In 1969, our last child was born—a healthy, sweet baby girl, Loretta, my fourth Caesarean birth, with a hysterectomy. But I was not well. Four Caesarean surgeries were more than my body could take.

My daughter Lorelei was to be confirmed the weekend after I came home. Even though the doctor strongly urged against it, Dave's family wanted to have a party for her. Of course we had the party. Neither Dave nor his family would listen to me, or to what the doctor said, and they promised they would handle everything. The house was full of people, so I did not get much rest and quiet. My mother stayed on to help me with the children.

The next day, I started to hemorrhage, as if a faucet had been turned on. Dave came home to drive me to the hospital, and while doctors were being paged STAT[19] for me, he said his goodbyes. I was so angry, I summoned enough strength to shout at him, "You mean that you would leave me lying here bleeding to death while they are calling doctors STAT for me! Go!" I suddenly wanted him gone. I didn't want him near me in my hour of death, for surely I was dying. Then my strength was gone. As he left, the doctors took over, and Jesus took me out of my body to a place that was pure, white and full of light. The release from my mortal self was beyond words. From this other dimension, I looked down on the doctors and saw them removing huge blood clots from me, and the floor and the doctors were covered in bright red blood. All else—the room, instruments, nurses, doors —all were shining white.

I so . . . did not want to go back into that body! But I had no choice that I knew of, and in anguish my spirit sang to God for release. I cannot begin to tell you how I felt, for even heaven would not have me. And Jesus, ever-near, said to me, *"Bear with us a little while."*

I replied with words that seemed foreign to me—as if coming from another plane—"When is my end, that I should be so patient?" Jesus spread his mantle over me and I slept.

* * *

I missed my children and worried about my new daughter during the seven days I was hospitalized. On the sixth day, I phoned my in-laws. None of Dave's family knew I was back in the hospital! Thinking back, I don't remember seeing Dave until it was time to go home. My mother stayed on another week to help with the children, two of them mere babies.

Dave ran for president of the UAW union in his workplace and did his politicking in the taverns, so he rarely came home for dinner or in time to play with the children. His idea of being a good father was to wake the children late at night to play with them, after being in the bar, or to drive around in the car with them and drink beer, and to buy them all the penny candy they wanted.

His drinking problem was serious, but he didn't think he was an alcoholic from just drinking beer. His family didn't give it much thought either, because every social occasion with his family included alcohol. And even though he drank at those gatherings, he did not mistreat me in front of his family.

> Your partner can be very loving in public, yet is short on care or consideration when you are alone together.[20]

He won the election. He would tell me that his abuse was the norm and I was lucky he wasn't worse, like some of the cases he had to deal with as president of the union.

> Family violence kills as many women every 5 years as the total number of Americans who died in the Vietnam War.[21]

I often had black eyes I had to hide, and one time we visited his family for an event and I just happened to have one of those black eyes. I had to lie about how I got it.

There were breaths of fresh air when I left Dave a few other times to live with his mother, for my parents did not have room for us. It was a reprieve for us, a time for me to heal. I loved his mother. She was a saint. As usual, he would find a way to convince me to come back.

He was fired from the UAW position within the year for misappropriating funds. I never could figure that out, since I was not aware of extra money coming into our home. However, just prior to this, he acquired a girlfriend and was absent for longer periods of time, so he may have used the extra money for her. Although I was taking care of our home and children, according to him I deserved nothing and everything was his, for he was the one who worked. His words often were, "Nothing is yours. It is all mine."

He was put back on the assembly line in the plant. I rarely saw his paycheck. He controlled what money he gave me for groceries and the bills he thought should be paid. I was afraid to answer the phone because of the many bill collectors calling. For years, the ringing of the phone caused me distress. My extra spending money was what I could garner from using coupons. I saved that money for the kids for school needs and to buy material to make them Christmas presents—clothing, Barbie doll clothes, and other presents. I bought wool coats from Goodwill and took them apart to make coats for the children.

And out of nowhere, just before Christmas, Dave suddenly would have plenty of money and would buy them lots of toys. Naturally, the children were happier with toys. This always made me feel smaller.

I was beginning to feel lost. I didn't turn to Jesus as much. I am not sure I had the strength to think past one moment to the next. I reserved enough strength to take care of the children and did little else. I knew I was giving up. I felt a darkness about me and couldn't seem to bring myself up from its depth. Living without inner power, I was laden with depression. It was like being in a womb without the nurturing. Thinking I had permanently messed up my life, I felt unworthy to acknowledge Jesus, even though He was always near.

For some time, I no longer wholly liked myself. If you asked my name, I would slur it all into one sound. I had hardly any feelings about most everything. I felt empty. Everything that I had thought was *me* was gone.

During this low ebb in my life, I was invited to go with some women to a day retreat. Dave gave his permission. It was a lovely retreat, and we each had our own small room for rest and contemplation.

Once in my room, I got on my knees and praised God for all that is good in the world, nature mostly, and for

Jesus in my life. It felt contrived to me, just familiar words with no heart. I tried to make it meaningful, genuine, but I couldn't bring forth the feelings. If I couldn't praise God, how could I possibly ask for anything? Still, on and on I tried to pray.

Then I turned from God to Jesus. I babbled to Him as I did when, as a child, I first knew Him. He felt as near as day and as far as the dark, night sky. Long into the afternoon I talked to Him, not expecting anything, and then my heart talk turned into lamentations, which rose to a crescendo, spilling forth all the pain, sorrow, shame and nothingness that I had been experiencing for what seemed like forever.

Strangely, feeling was being restored in me, for I had finally opened myself to Jesus, something I had been unable to do. Yet, no answers that I was settled enough to hear came forth. Exhausted, sleep overtook me.

In the evening, I reluctantly went with the others as they all gathered in a large room. A priest led us in what he called "creative visualization." He lowered the lights and asked us to close our eyes. In soothing words, He told us to imagine we were in a favorite place, relaxing. I imagined I was at the family cottage, lounging outside under the trees. He then told us to imagine Jesus was walking toward us. That was easy. He came out of the woods toward me. The priest then said, "Jesus is going to talk to you. What does He say?"

Suddenly, time seemed to stand still. Then, in a voice

booming with force from out of a whisper, Jesus slowly, seemingly taking all of eternity, audibly said to me, "*MARY ANN . . . I LOVE YOU.*"

I gasped, drew in His words, and they entered every particle of my being—filled me past full. I looked into Jesus' eyes. They were shining lights—like water sparkling in the sun—as when, at the age of five, I first saw Him. I sensed they held everything about my existence, present and future, within their gaze. His eyes seemed to be smiling. And, as if for the first time, I simply knew, in the eyes of Jesus, that I was not worthless, insignificant and nothing. I felt renewed.

I never slurred my name again.

Truly, He was there for everyone in that room, each receiving what they needed to hear and feel. And truly, Jesus is there for all, even in the darkest of days and nights, and hears you even if you don't hear him.

Rarely did Dave show his colors in front of his family. One weekend, one of his sisters and her husband came to stay with us overnight, and he didn't come home. He forgot they were coming. The next morning, I called a buddy of his, and he said he would get with Dave. Dave came home in time to say goodbye to his sister. His sister never questioned where he had been.

I decided that I had had enough and bravely told Dave I was leaving for good. I started packing everything I could into the car. With four kids in tow, I left.

Women are most likely to be killed when attempting to leave the abuser. In fact, they're at a 75% higher risk than those who stay.[22]

It was odd that he didn't object this time.

We didn't go to Dave's mother. We went to my parents, room or no room. Dave had second thoughts and came for me, and I refused to go back to living with him. In spite of my refusal, he took sick leave claiming a bad back, and moved from our trailer in Vassar into a garage next to the burned-out house, to be nearby. I was afraid having him so close.

Choices[23], a current program in Michigan, offers alternatives to people living in violent situations.

He worked on me through the children. I knew he loved them. How could I deny him the children? It was too crowded in my parents' small apartment, and I had no other choices at that time. He sweet-talked me into believing all would be well, and I gave up, resigned and took him back. I was sure I could be a stronger person this time and not take his abuse. Even though Dave had not won my trust and I was still afraid of him, I had to believe that all would work out in the end.

Instilled in my heart were Jesus words, *"Soon, fear will take leave from you."*

So I had reason to believe all would be well.

We moved into the garage—all six of us. Dave and I had one bed, and three other children were in the same room on bunk beds. Linda had her own little room. Our bathroom was an outhouse.

I was never given free time away from the children to take a ride by myself or visit a friend or visit my parents alone.

Dave was diagnosed with diabetes, but he continued to drink and did not monitor himself well. It was disheartening to watch him go downhill.

The woodpile behind the wood stove caught fire one night. Dave had filled the stove with wood, enough to last through the night. There were a lot of holes in the stove, and the extra air fed the fire, so the stove was always blazing hot. I was on strong tranquilizers and I would sleep soundly. Loretta woke me up. I saw the room lit up with light from the dancing flames and I screamed. Dave woke from a deep sleep and immediately screamed at me, "Now what did you do?", always accusing. I got the children out and he put the fire out. From then on, during that winter, I slept on the couch, tended the fire myself, and put one log at a time on the fire throughout each long winter night.

If the abuser never accepts fault and responsibility when things go wrong, be ready to be blamed for anything.[24]

One day, I decided to go into the barn to clean up some things the previous owners left. I rarely went into the barn at all. I was drawn to a cabinet and opened it and picked up a dusty bottle, one of many. The label said "arsenic" . . . large tablets that I later learned are given to cattle to make them throw up. My immediate thought was, "This is how I'm going to do it!" My subconscious mind wanted me to kill my husband, and I hadn't even been aware of it! The thought tore through my soul like a knife. Something shifted in me, I could feel it. I couldn't seem to move. I couldn't go backward, and I couldn't go forward, and I couldn't stay where I was. I felt I was on the edge of something critical. From then on, it took effort to function and I battled between my lower self and my higher self. I was terrified that I might poison him.

I begged Jesus to not leave my side and to monitor every move I made. At mealtimes I didn't feel I could trust myself, so I concentrated on preparing Dave only one food item at a time. I worried about what I might do and what else my subconscious might come up with. I didn't feel in control anymore. I became ill and couldn't eat. I couldn't lift a laundry basket. I knew I was in trouble. I needed to get help. I needed to be away from him. I didn't want to kill him. The thought devastated me. I thought I was truly losing my mind. How could I possibly think of killing anyone?

> Prison terms for killing husbands are twice as long as for killing wives. And 93% of women who killed their mates had been physically and/or emotionally battered by them.[25]

For a long time, I had felt as if I were unimportant to Dave. He had told me over and over that nothing was mine including the children, and that I was nothing. I knew he loved the children, and I felt sure they would be taken care of and I could just disappear, go to Jesus. Everyone would be safer that way.

> Subject to their control they may treat you as a piece of property, to do with as they please. Words are used to brainwash.[26]

I turned to Jesus and fell on my knees, pleading for help . . . pleading for Him to take me from all of this, for I was now my own worst enemy. He said to me:

"Just a little while, and this suffering will be no more. For it will soon fade like grass in winter."

Jesus' words gave me a glimmer of hope, and I reached out for help. I went to my doctor and tried to get him to admit me into a mental hospital. He wouldn't, but he increased the dosages on my tranquilizers! From there I sought help from a counselor; I crumbled in his office, collapsed. When I gathered myself and could communicate, he said it would be better for me to admit myself, so I could discharge myself if I wanted to leave. My dear mother drove me, and I admitted myself into a mental hospital.

I was nearly catatonic and felt devoid of life. I was as low as one can possibly feel and still be alive. A psychiatrist questioned me; I responded little. He then took me to a private bedroom, left, and locked the door behind him.

"Oh, Sweet Jesus, only you know how safe I felt behind those locked doors. It was as if a great burden lifted from me. And when you held me, I felt I would never leave there."

Wrapped safely in the arms of Jesus, I slept for hours.

Up to 64% of hospitalized female psychiatric patients have histories of being physically abused as adults.[27]

I wore sunglasses until they took them away from me, for I could not meet anyone's eyes looking into mine. There was no anger in me. No anger toward God or Jesus or even Dave. There was no feeling.

I could see a constant pinpoint of light—far in the distance as if at the end of a dark tunnel—which I simply believed was God.

I isolated myself as much as they would allow me to, and I couldn't eat. It was mandatory to eat in the dining room, and they checked the dishes to be sure the food had been eaten. I immediately knew what I had to do. I would fill my tray with dishes of food and go to the back of the dining room, where there were several patients, and trade full dishes for empty ones with eager recipients. I never got caught, and the patients shared my secret with me. I never ate for the month that I was there; I just drank juice.

After the first few days, they made me leave my room during the day and go to the sunroom. A piano was in the center of the room. I went to it, sat down, and there before me was a classical music book for piano, similar to one I had used in my teens. I started at the beginning of the book and played, like a robot, from front to back. Then I shut the book and went to my room.

Daily I secluded and abandoned myself in the music—an escape that brought me peace and gave me comfort. After a week of playing the same things over and over, someone came along with a popular music book, and I played it from front to back. Before I knew it, people would surround the piano and point out things they wanted to hear. I was told "the crazies" upstairs settled down when I played. I didn't like that expression. I wondered how many of them were like me. From then on, I consciously played for them. I never sang while there.

Initially, I could not imagine, from out of the depths of the void, what kind of life I could have out in the world again, nor did I give it much thought. My only concern was for my children; the future was in God's hands. Still, with Jesus ever present in my consciousness, I never felt alone. And now I had my music. No one could rob me of either.

Every day was a dichotomy, as if I were two people: part of me was blissful, living in the present moment, but the other, my earthly thoughts and emotions, not always pleasant. Painful memories, fears, uncertain thoughts of the future, flitted through my mind as if they were passing, burning embers on the wind. Only Jesus kept me whole.

A psychiatrist unrelentingly questioned me about the supposed affair Dave was always accusing me of. I wasn't free from Dave's influence anywhere. I could see in the counselor's eyes that he was unsure whether to believe me or not, for I was the one in a mental hospital. He reminded me of the old priest who implied I was less than Dave and should simply get used to it.

There were things I wanted to say, needed to say, yet I felt pained, as if once again attacked. I couldn't answer him, to trust the truth of my innocence to such as he. There were no female counselors to speak to, and I began to wonder how I could get help in a place like this.

All my life, until my encounter with the priest and this counselor, the patriarchal control that permeates society lay almost completely unrecognized as such by me. I had adapted to it, and only now did I realize that it wasn't just in my husband. My eyes were opened to the threat to all that is feminine . . . to my own daughters.

Back in my room, I turned to Jesus, who had never made me feel angry, or inferior as a woman. He wrapped me in His mantle. No words were necessary. Safely, my angry thoughts flowed, fast and furious like a turbulent river; then just as swiftly, my whole being—mind and body and spirit—settled into the great lake of sleep.

Dave wrote to me and said, "How could you do this to my family?", never thinking about me as a person nor his part in all that had happened.

Dave admitted himself to the mental hospital where I was. I felt this was to get at me, though he did need help. I later learned the children were divided up and cared for by his relatives. The hospital staff tried to keep Dave and me apart. One day, I saw him down a hall and the fear came back. I had been feeling safer than I could even remember, and then there he was and fear hit me like a ton of bricks. I ran into a room where he couldn't get to me. When he realized he couldn't get at me, he checked out.

In group therapy, I finally opened up to talking about wanting to kill my husband and they all laughed. Nearly everyone had seriously wanted to kill someone at some time. I couldn't fathom it.

I was not well. I would sweat profusely. It poured off of me, drenching anything used to wipe it away. The psychiatrist called it hyperhidrosis, stimulated by my emotional response to my situation. It left me exhausted.

Dave, in the meantime, had received temporary custody of the children, because I was in the "crazy house", as he called it. Once, he brought the children and my brother to see me. Linda had asthma and looked terrible. My brother later told me that, when they left after visiting me, Dave drove like a mad man, putting all of them in danger. I was at a loss as to what to do about it. I was not strong enough to go back to that situation. Concern for Linda and the other children haunted my days.

Ah, blessed children,
you who suffered needlessly
with those who did not speak of love,
I prayed for you and your father in the silence.

* * *

The one person I grew to trust was a psychologist. Upon telling him some of my problems, he told me I did not deserve this. That was like opening a door, giving me permission to own freedom. I rolled those words over and over in my mind. They became my mantra: "I do not deserve this, I do not deserve this." I resolved to free myself from Dave's control, and I slowly became stronger.

Dave served me with divorce papers, just what I had wanted for a long time. I was getting help where I was. I was eligible for tuition for college through a Vocational Rehabilitation program.

When I was finally released, after being there a month, I went to see a lawyer, and he advised me to get an apartment for the children and myself to show that I could provide a home for them. It was through the constant presence of Jesus in my heart that I brought forth the inner strength needed to follow through, for I was still very afraid of my husband.

While awaiting the divorce and custody trial, Dave continued to keep the children, but I was granted visitation. There was nothing more I could do.

Dave insisted that I drive out into the country to pick the children up. The first time I went to get them, he used them to try to convince me to come back. With pleading looks on the children's faces, it was so hard to say "no." When I wouldn't give in, he got mad and put his hands around my neck to choke me. All the children piled on top of him to stop him. I fled from the house. Then he would not let me take them with me. He deliberately stood in front of my car while he held our son, David. I drove forward slowly to get him to move. I was scared of him. I called my lawyer, and from then on, he had to deliver the children to me. He told his lawyer that I tried to run him and David over!

> When spouse abuse is considered, divorced or separated men committed 79% of the assaults.[28]

The court date for finalization of the divorce and custody suit was nearing. Dave toted a gun and waved it around at others. Even my parents were afraid for their lives.

> Weapons are an extension of self. A person is what he/she lives. If he ever "playfully" points a gun at you or ever gestures at you with another weapon, what could happen if he became very angry with you?[29]

I received a phone call one day from Lorelei, warning me to leave the house. She had observed Dave putting a gun in a potato chip bag, and she knew he was coming to see me. She was afraid he would shoot me. I left the house with my friend Patricia, who was visiting me. While I was gone, he broke into the house, did some damage and left. I called my lawyer and the police. If this happened today and I had a restraining order in place, they would have picked him up. Back then, nothing could be done until he actually hurt someone!

> Of females killed with a firearm, almost two-thirds were killed by their intimate partners.[30]

A cousin of mine had business with Dave's lawyer and was there for an appointment and saw Dave leave. My cousin told the lawyer what he knew of the situation. The lawyer was appalled by what was said, because he had been led to believe some terrible things about me. He called Dave, and as a result, Dave went berserk and left the children.

By the following day, the children had been left alone for over twenty-four hours, and then they started making phone calls, looking for their father. I wasn't home; I was visiting my parents. Linda told me that one aunt she had called said, "He'll be alright, don't worry, bye now." They called everyone they could think of, including another aunt, who went looking for Dave. Finally Dave went home and asked the children, "Who wants to go and live with your mother?" Both Lorelei and Loretta fearfully raised their hands.

Our son, David, couldn't raise his hand. I remember, when David would come to visit, he would be wearing layers of clothing—two pairs of socks and pants, and layers of shirts and underwear. He hoped his father would not notice and that he could stay with me if he had extra clothing. He was only six years old. In my heart, I knew he was afraid of his father. We all were.

Linda had not responded to her father's question, because she simply wanted to run away from all of it and not be with either of us.

Dave brought Lorelei and Loretta to my house and left them sitting on my doorsteps. I wasn't home. He dropped

David off somewhere else. I received a phone call at my parents' apartment to tell me that my children were sitting on my doorstep.

Dave phoned me at my home later and said, "Well, tomorrow everything will be yours." His remark that everything would be mine was out of character for Dave. Not like him at all. I called my neighbors, friends of his, to go and check on Dave, and they said they would follow through.

Later, our son, David, was dropped off at my house. Linda was at my brother-in-law's house, and I went to get her. She said her father was going to commit suicide. I told her he was too chicken. She argued with me and didn't want to come. She finally agreed. Years later, Linda apologized to me and told me she came with me because she thought I was unstable and would need help caring for the other children. Now she knew better. Her apology touched my heart.

None of us had control over a momentum of events that seemed to keep building. It was like a volcano getting ready to erupt. You feel something is going to happen, you just don't know what or when. Everything was moving too fast.

I remember asking Jesus to let happen what is best for all of us.

And these words exploded in my heart, *"Remember this: It is written in the stars and shines over the land that you have mastery over your own soul destiny, even if God intervenes in your mortal existence."*

Then I knew God had taken over.

The next day was the bicentennial Fourth of July. The children and I decided to go on a picnic with my brother and his wife. We truly needed to do something to take our minds off our worries. Upon arriving at their house, we had to wait for my brother, who was off on an errand. When he came home, he told us that Dave had committed suicide.

And I remembered Jesus' prophetic words, *"Just a little while and this suffering will be no more. For it will soon fade like grass in winter."*

Chapter Five

Somewhere In Time

"Let children walk with Nature, let them see the beautiful blendings and communions of death and life, their joyous inseparable unity, as taught in woods and meadows, plains and mountains and streams of our blessed star, and they will learn that death is stingless indeed, and as beautiful as life."

—John Muir

Upon hearing of Dave's death, the wind was knocked out of me. I felt like a wilted flower, momentarily detached from emotion. And yet my children were seated before me and they needed me. I could not abandon them. I gasped for breath and instantly, from deep within my heart, called out to Jesus for help. His voice came from the depths of the ocean and as high as forever. He simply said,

"You have tarried too long in this place."

As my soul swayed, confused, between the past and future, in this one instant of time, life was instilled into my heart. The veil was lifted from my darkness, light found its way into my hidden, inner self, and I was made strong.

I took my children up, and over the rainbow we went, into the land of somewhere in time, where we could hear the rush of humanity and be a part of it. Hand in hand, the children and I faced the big, scary world. And I knew the sacredness of life was still there, somewhere.

Oh . . . the myriad of affects we experienced together, back then, in varying shades of light! Loss was reawakened each time death was spoken of by extended family and friends. For how could anyone's death be anything but a loss to someone?

Freedom now, at this exorbitant price, unfettered our conditioned minds, bodies, and souls, so much so that we only politely listened to others and then found peace at home, where we rarely spoke of what had happened.

And, if the children had any memory of happiness with their father, I did not want to crush it with my negativity. Nor did I want them to remind me of their father.

For thirty years, until the writing of this book, we rarely discussed him. But now, these many years later, I can see what a blessing it is to break the silence that kept our tender sensibilities caged, to share and compare with my children and others our personal reflections as adults, candidly without bitterness, and to bring closure to that part of our past. It has brought my children and me ever-closer together as a family.

Through the years, I have often thought about the wonderful events in our children's lives that Dave missed out on and for which the children have not had a Dad. Sometimes, I also think that, if I had been strong enough to leave him in the beginning, he might be alive today.

My son, David, let me know that he desperately wanted to come to me when his father gave him the choice, but he was too afraid of his father to say so. It felt like layers of sadness were being lifted from David as he said this.

Lorelei told me she feels her father is sorry for everything he did and is now helping her from wherever he is. It was she who alerted me to the danger of being shot and may have saved my life.

Loretta remembers little, but enough to remind me that it was she who woke in time to save all of us from fire.

I pray that when bad memories come, my children can simply say, "Be gone!" and release them.

Without my steadfast faith and trust in God and Jesus, I would not have been able to endure the abusive suppression. For every time I fell into despair, Jesus endeavored to pick me up. Every time I doubted my ability to continue, He made His presence known in my heart, fortified me, and gave me hope. In the worst of times, I saw Jesus' face superimposed on Dave's, and would be able to separate myself from the abuse by leaving my body. I felt God's protection then and knew Dave could only wound my mortal self. My soul was hidden from him. And, too, I marvelled at how my intuition and reasoning revealed impending abuse so I could try to avoid it.

You may wonder why I allowed the abusive relationship to continue. I was afraid of what Dave might do to my children and myself if I left him for good. At the time, in the 1960's and 70's, I had never heard of protective services, and they may not even have been available. Staying with him held slim hope for the future; leaving, I felt, held even less hope for safe existence, for me and the children.

Did our marriage serve a purpose? I have four beautiful children and their families as a result of that marriage, for which I am grateful. Perhaps it taught the children and me something we needed for the growth of our souls. The experience certainly has deepened my understanding of others in similar situations.

I would advise anyone to leave an abusive situation and not go back as I did, children or no children. To such a person, I would say: "Look inward; look at why you stay in your situation. Do you believe your situation can or cannot be repaired? Do you think you deserve what is happening to you? No one deserves abuse.

It is easy for me to say this in retrospect. However, I think in this day and age, with Internet, television, and other modern resources, one could more easily find support to mend or get out of an abusive relationship. Help can be found through doctors, hospitals, churches, mental health counselors, libraries, schools and in the phone book under "Protective Services." Recently I saw a poster, in a women's restroom stall, indicating where help could be found! Keep searching until you find the kind of assistance you need.

For me, I was never aware of any resources. The only constant in my life was God and my friendship with Jesus. This realization never wavered.

Ever present, Jesus is now saying to me, *"Brave Heart, the end days of your marriage were taken out of your hands, God directed. You initiated it through your absolute surrender in God. People were then placed in your path, and events that were ordained to happen for your highest good were manifested."*

"Oh, how I know. Everything changed the day my deep, subconscious said to me, 'This is how I will do it', in regard to the arsenic I found in the barn. I could not fathom the implication. I could not kill anyone. I was afraid of the darkness. I surrendered it all to God, and yet this required a different surrendering from when as a healer I initially said to God, 'Use me as you will.'

"This time my surrender encompassed my whole being, the light and the dark; it had to. Once I committed myself to unconditional surrender, I found my very essence, physical and nonphysical, dissolving into God, as if I were blending into infinity . . . losing my self-will, giving up to God. This was neither blissful nor non-blissful; it simply was.

"But, did my surrendering in God lead to Dave's death?"

"There were other choices for him."

"Deep down I knew that, Sweet Jesus. It quiets my heart when you take feelings of guilt from me, for I wonder at times if he might have wanted me to feel guilty."

"There you are. . . . Stop doing this to yourself; you don't deserve it."

"Thank you, Sweet Jesus!"

I hope my story will help heal those who have experienced abuse, give hope to those who are being abused, and keep others from making the same mistakes I made. Most of all, I hope what I have shared will demonstrate that God is as close to you as the air you breathe and, when we suffer, God has not abandoned us.

My daughter Linda summed it up this way, "After everything, you never put him down to us. You didn't dredge up that he beat you and ran around. It wasn't talked about; it was over. Sad to say, I think we all felt a sense of relief. You mentioned something about him missing events in our lives; I think many of those events might not have happened. Can you imagine him allowing me to have a boyfriend? I wonder if I would have gone to college. I went to college because I refused to have to depend on someone. Finding a good husband along the way was a bonus."

Like a whisper of wind, the thought came to me that it

was more than the word "bonus" could ever hold. I simply said to her, "No, it was a gift."

Each member of my immediate family is, in their own way, a gift to each other and to others. We are well aware of this blessing as we work together as a family. We reprimand, we make up, we honor; above all, we love.

Chapter Six

Life

One day at a time is sufficient
to fulfill a dream.

Family and friends didn't know how to approach us after Dave died. I could see their awkwardness in their mannerisms and faces. And I, too, didn't know what to say to comfort them in their discomfort. There should be a book giving proper speaking etiquette for sickness, death, first dates, or to break a silence, with simple sentences to memorize in case you might need them. But I have never found such a book.

I could have dwelt on the past and chosen bitterness, but instead gratefulness filled my life. I gave thanks to Jesus and God in quiet moments of contemplation throughout the day, which awakened blissful feelings within me. Peace took the place of fear.

The children were changed also, for how could they not change with breaths of fresh air filling our home and goodness filling our lives, as they slowly unburdened their grief.

Sometimes tragedy brings out the best in us. For now, propelled by relief from fear, happiness began to slip in as if it had been waiting outside to come in or was peeking at us from around a corner and wanted to pounce on us unexpectedly. We began to learn to laugh when it touched us. We took a trip to Disney World and laughed even more.

I didn't have a difficult transition financially, as most widowed or divorced parents have. There was social security for the children, and I worked. I didn't need Medicaid. I was fully capable of budgeting, and now bills got paid, old and new, including funeral expenses. My schooling was mostly covered by a rehabilitation program. There was just enough, yet it was more money than I had ever had.

When the first social security check came in, I took the children to the grocery store, gave each of them a cart, and told them to fill it. I gave them all the time they needed. They ranged in age from five to fifteen years old. What fun we had! Each ended up with their own stash and also purchased items for household needs according to what they felt was important.

Within a year, I had a modest home built with proceeds from Dave's life insurance and the sale of our trailer, plus a mortgage. Some people thought it was my parent's money that allowed me to do what I did. They bought me a used car, but I did the rest and was proud of what I could do.

I had not been in a position to have many friends before Dave's death. And now I found my few married friends didn't want a single mom in their midst. Private clubs closed their doors on me, as I needed to be the wife of a member to join. I wasn't ready for dating, but after a time of adjustment, I felt ready to spread my wings for the first time in seventeen years—to reach out and socialize without fear of reprisal—but where? Only the taverns in town welcomed single women!

The church offered few activities that the children and I could take part in together. We spent time at the beach and with my parents—their grandparents. After summer they had school activities. I began to play the pipe organ at Guardian Angel Church for all the masses and funerals and started singing again. I auditioned for a part in a musical at the Ramsdell Theater, and ended up doing many musicals, most often as female lead. I loved to sing. I loved the theater, and it fulfilled my social needs.

Eventually, I felt ready to date other men. It was a time of relationships—another taste of life. Dave had been the only man I knew intimately.

I had gone back to the Lutheran church I attended as a child. Religion for me is a way to be with God, and God is everywhere and in all things. So, for me, going from the Lutheran to Catholic to Lutheran faith was a simple matter, for I saw divinity in all religions that worship God and didn't pay much attention to their individual doctrines. But confessing to a priest, knowing that I could go straight to God, didn't make sense to me.

When I called my brother-in-law, Father John, to inform him of my decision, he hesitated and then said to me, "Remember this, I am going to heaven in a Cadillac and you might have to take an Oldsmobile!" And that is all he said on the matter.

I began going to college, with help through the vocational rehabilitation program. I also worked and cared for the children.

Four years passed before I married again. I had four children; Don had six. Since his children had a mother and some were on their own, we did not have all of his children living with us. And my daughter Linda was off at college. Our relationship was one of love and mutual respect.

Don was good to me. I thought this marriage would be good for all of us, but the challenge of mixing families is often difficult. The children were not always happy, and they played us against each other.

Our means of disciplining were different. My children were expected to do their share of chores, while his rarely had to do anything. My children reluctantly went to church on Sunday, and Don and his children seldom went. I felt it all-important for my children to attend Sunday school and services. It was the best way I could think of to instill in them Jesus' teachings, for children don't always listen to parents.

Don did not understand my relationship with Jesus. In a gentle way, he let me know he did not want to talk of his nor my faith. I felt bad that he did not want to share his beliefs with me, and there was much I wanted to share with him. All I could do was instill love in him by loving him.

Although we loved each other, his love excluded my children. It broke my heart, for I wanted a father—a real father—for my children. He displayed an interest in them prior to our marriage, but it soon faded. Even after they grew up and left home, Don resented their visits. It was almost as if he wanted me all to himself. I would become upset because of his apathy toward my children.

My family found him hard to be around. We finally gave up expecting him to take part in family gatherings. I said to the children, "That's just Don," and we let it go at that. When the family gathered in our house, he would isolate himself in another room.

Don was never abusive and would do anything for me. He was not a drinker nor did he run around. He was the one who maintained our investment properties. He was an electrician and would do whatever needed doing that he was capable of. He was a hard worker and, sick or not, always went to work. We enjoyed short trips together. He supported me when I wanted to continue college.

I was already nearing completion of an associate's degree when I married Don. It took me four years, part-time, to complete the two-year course I had enrolled in at West Shore Community Collge. From there I started classes at Grand Valley State University. I loved academic life. At the end of my junior year, I applied for Western Michigan University's occupational therapy program. It was very competitive, but my grades were impressive and, being in a minority because of my age, I was admitted into their program. First, I spent the summer at Grand Valley in intensive study, fulfilling prerequisites, and then completed two full-time years of occupational therapy at Western, plus a year of internships.

Jesus was always there for me. He was my best-kept secret. Secret, because I wanted to fit in and people just didn't understand my relationship with Jesus when I talked of it. A conventional faith in Jesus was what they knew, and they couldn't fathom a personal relationship in which Jesus could be with me (or anyone else) every moment of every day.

Sometimes I didn't want to continue my education, for being a full-time student was harder than part-time. Also, it was not easy leaving my husband, children, and even grandchildren behind for most of the week, then returning home to attend to family needs on a three-day weekend.

It was a three-hour trip to Western from home, and Jesus was often in the seat next to me, especially when I was overwhelmed with studying or felt like giving up. Communing with Jesus and laying all my troubles and cares on Him as I drove cleared my mind and gave me the strength to go on. By the time I would reach my destination, I was newly energized and ready to continue.

Breath work helped me study, too. I could breathe in love-filled energy and send it throughout my very being, including my brain, to keep my mind clearer and in better form for study. My brain was not as resilient as a twenty-year old's.

I was part of a study group, which met often. They would sit around a table, and I would be on my feet, pacing. Every once in a while, after listening to them, I would say, "Have you thought of this?" or "Did you ever consider doing it this way?" For some reason, some of them thought I was brilliant, when in fact my mind was simply very clear.

I never sang at Western until I had to give a presentation in a sign-language class. The assignment was to use sign to interpret a song. So, while using sign, I sang harmony with Barry Manilow's CD recording of *When October Goes.* I blew them away, for the sound bounded off the walls and windows and filled them. It truly brought my grade up in a class that was hard for me. I am soft-spoken but can project magnificently while singing.

I felt like I was driven or on a mission to fulfill a desire for an education, and after many years of college, including internships, I graduated from Western Michigan University as an occupational therapist, at the age of fifty-one. Truly, one day at a time is sufficient to fulfill a dream.

When my four children and Don's youngest child were grown and on their own, and I was finally settled into an occupational therapy job, Don and I remodeled a warehouse into a home for ourselves, with additional rental units.

Situated on the Manistee River at the western end of downtown Manistee, a port city in lower Michigan, our home was also in view of Lake Michigan. The river flowed alongside of the riverwalk, just below our windows. It was Christmas, 1993, when we finally moved in.

What a beautiful Christmas that was! Our tree was magnificent, twelve feet tall with hundreds of miniature lights, covered with homemade and gifted ornaments and an abundance of glittery, golden snowflakes. A beautiful, blue angel topped it off. As you walked into the front entrance, you could see straight into the great room, where the tree was; and then, through an expanse of glass, lay the river and Lake Michigan. There were many tall windows in the great room, framed by deep emerald-green walls, bringing the wintry snow scene indoors.

The base of the tree was strewn with gifts of all shapes and sizes. A doll, representing baby Jesus, lay amongst the gifts, wrapped in His blanket, waiting for the grandchildren to hold Him carefully and rock Him; and so did I.

We kept the tree up well into January because of its beauty. The setting made us feel as if we were in a world of our own—our dream come true.

One evening, toward the end of that January, to celebrate a birthday early, my husband and I went out to eat. We were ecstatically happy that evening. We had finally made the decision to sit back and enjoy our new home, which we had only one month before moved into and had worked so hard and so long to build. We decided to put things on hold for a while.

As we enjoyed our dinner, we began to relax. He wanted a dinner roll that I left on my plate and I told him it would cost him a kiss. He got up in the busy restaurant, came around the table and kissed me passionately. I gave him the roll.

It was as if a breeze of fresh air had come through us and taken away the sense of needing to get things done yesterday, of never having free time for today. We talked of taking a trip, getting in a car and just going to see how far a week would take us, with a week to get back, and choices of directions to go. We spoke of visiting his children downstate. He spoke of going fishing more often. We spoke of just sitting back and enjoying life.

It was a lovely evening and a lovely dinner. And when we arrived home, walking in the door of our new home, we remarked to each other how warm and lovely it was and how it felt so comfortable—so ours.

The next morning, he died at work. . . .

FAREWELL

Oh, such wonderful, well-laid plans
vanquished by death of a loved man.
Why bother at all my mind complains,
as my heartfelt grieving reigns.

With shattered dreams I now am caged,
as my mourning days are waged.
"Jesus, tell me, where is my death?"
"You are God's own, stayed with breath."

A spark of hope within His tone . . .
blessed solace now is this alone:
Jesus, my comforter and my guide,
shows me, o'er every moment
God does preside.

Chapter Seven

New Horizons

THE HEALER

The healer sometimes fails, sometimes falls,
and from that falling, ascends, grows, and leaves
the intellectual warp behind, if for only a moment,
and in that moment becomes healed.

Ego plays its vain part within the scene,
puffing up with emptiness,
while God is set aside.

Prayer throws the ego out a
window of see-through glass
and clouds it over to keep it out.
Prayer is . . . being alone now with God.

The healer and God, being alone,
become melded into oneness.
With God, the healer becomes whole . . .
renewed . . .

until a new falling away,
and from that falling, ascends, grows, and leaves
the intellectual warp behind, if for only a moment,
and in that moment becomes healed.

I was alone then. The children were grown and gone. I grieved for what seemed like an eternity, a grief unlike anything I had ever experienced or read about. I lost strength and often felt breathless. My daughter Lorelei and her two children, Justin and Allysha, came to live with me to help me through it all. Still, I never lost sight of God, and Jesus comforted me when I would let Him. Sometimes I simply wanted to grieve. I found value in the grief. Grief is not like a tissue pulled out of a box, the same every time for everyone.

Nature echoed my emotions. In my journal I wrote:

The mighty lake pounds the pier
in concert with my beating heart.
Clouds congregate in turbulent groups.
Water pours from the sky.

Then suddenly, one day in September of 1994, eight months after Don had passed, I was done with grieving—as if I had awakened from a bad dream. I am not sure if it was a conscious decision on my part or if God granted an end to the grief. Further, I decided to take to the road as a traveling occupational therapist. Lorelei and her children moved back home.

When you take a traveling position, you work three-month settings in various parts of the country. I thoroughly cleaned and prepared my home before leaving for my first work assignment. As I entered my car to leave, I was suddenly compelled to go back into the house. I walked in,

looked into every room, then as I gazed out the windows—
looking at everything and seeing nothing—time stood still.

> *There exists a place . . .*
> *Between the nether and the ether . . .*
> *A fine line of demarcation.*
> *I went there to rest awhile.*

Then I said goodbye to my beloved river and my home.
Turning around at the door for one last look, I said aloud to
God, "I can die now."

Then Jesus words, *"You have tarried too long in this*
place," came back to me.

And with Jesus' words in my heart, there was no
hesitation in leaving behind my whole support system of
family and friends, and life as I had known it. I was being
born again into a new life, but I didn't realize it then.

The agency for traveling therapists set me up in an
apartment, half underground. It was stark, no television,
and I called it a nunnery. Seemed fitting, as I was relying
only on Jesus and God for companionship. Instead of
reaching out to socialize, I avoided all outside activity
except for when I had to go to work. I spent my time
studying occupational therapy theory, praying and talking
to Jesus. When asked where I lived, I would joke about my
nunnery.

Maybe my drive to learn was to make up for lost time.
Or perhaps being an occupational therapist was truly
becoming the missionary I had always wanted to be. I

didn't give it much thought. I had a job to do and I wanted
to learn as much as I could and I wanted to know it all
"now."

I remember one specific evening in my nunnery, as I
was standing at the kitchen sink, an unlikely place for what
was about to happen. I was looking out the window into the
black of night, washing some dishes and talking to Jesus
about my day. Suddenly, Jesus appeared and quickly
entered my heart. I felt a swelling of energy within me; a
warm smile spread throughout my whole being. It was
almost a physical thing, it was so purposeful and real. He
was no longer outside of me but within me.

I took a deep breath and held it for ever so long. I didn't
become Jesus; He had simply entered my heart.

There are words to a song that sum it all up: "Christ
within me, Christ behind me, Christ before me, Christ
beside me . . . "

And Jesus reminds me as I write this, *"Abide in me and
I in you . . . that you may allow the illumination and joy of
your unconscious be known to you with thankful grace, and
to accept, with trust and without question, by letting go and
letting God."*

You might wonder if such experiences made it difficult
for me to focus on activities of daily living. But it seemed
natural to me to consider all my activities as serving God,
even the mundane upkeep of my body and apartment.

At the beginning of my first work assignment, I was

intimidated by a know-it-all physical therapist. I shied away from him.

Then one day, Jesus said to me, *"There is much that lies hidden within his knowledge. Listen and learn."*

So instead of cowering in the background, I began to listen, asked questions, and shared what I knew about therapy.

One day at work, the physical therapist said to me, "I could feel your aura when you came into the room." I said, "My what?!" I had no clue what he was talking about. He told me that, when I was at home and relaxed in bed, I should reach out, then gently bring my hands in toward my body and try to feel differences in the air. "That," he said, "is the aura." That night I did what he said, and surprisingly, I found differences in the "air." Further, I was moved to smooth my aura out, and a backache I had been suffering with disappeared.

The therapist had more knowledge of spiritual healing to share. One thing led to another, and before I knew it, I was prayerfully smoothing out patients' auras. Healing was occurring in people! I was truly amazed at what was happening. It had been Sweet Jesus' sustaining presence that bade me to be still and listen to the therapist's words of wisdom—a catalyst for so much more.

Ever in my heart, Jesus is saying, *"And you took that wisdom and ran with it."*

"Ah Sweet Jesus, what can I say? What words can come

forth from my mouth that will express my joy, yet joy is that to which sorrow also clings. Is the sadness in our lives and those of our patients to give us something to compare to, so we recognize the blessings when they come? What adjustments can we make to achieve better balance in our lives?"

"There are infinite reasons for everything, Brave Heart. Within earth's duality you experience imbalances. It is in opening to one's true self that you open to God-realization, oneness.

"Stay strong. Do not deny your gift and you will enhance your life force, wherein you will find pure joy. For whatever you are filled with you pour."

Jesus seemed content with that, and the encounter faded, just as morning mist fades with the rising sun.

* * *

"Why me?" loomed in my mind. And then, not even waiting for an answer, the question became, "What do you want me to do now, Lord?" And again, without thinking, words poured forth in utmost surrender to God, "Use me as you will."

I dove into this healing role without even giving it much thought. I didn't have time to think. I had never in my wildest dreams ever considered that I might one day be a healer. Now, healing became my passion, opening up ever-new views of our illusive world. I could only trust that I would recognize God's guidance in all that I did.

Jesus instructed me not to study healing nor take classes and that the lessons would come from within myself and from Himself and God.

I don't want to imply that such study is not good. For it can reveal new vistas of knowledge and stimulate new visions and understandings of life. I think Jesus simply wanted me to awaken my ability to listen to my inner knowing and God.

Interesting, isn't it, that this healing gift would be made known to me when my children and husband were gone and I was away from my hometown and church support group and only had Jesus, God and myself to depend on. Up until then, I knew nothing about spiritual healing, although I had seen faith healers on television.

Now that I was widowed, alone and on traveling work assignments, I was free to grow into my role as a healer—free from the influence of others' expectations—free to be me. I marveled at what I found. And I became more and more aware of and sensitive to God's energy within all things in the world.

I always knew that the essence of a godly life lies in the way we live our life. And I realized that being a healer did not take away from the essence of my life, but rather, enhanced it.

Since my first three-month assignment was only three hours away from my hometown, I was able to go home on some weekends and attend the church that I went to prior to leaving town.

I always had a role in this church. I was a follower. I did what was asked and expected of me and then some. I believed what everyone else believed. I could have opinions, but was expected to come around to the accepted norm.

I had been content with my religion and never found a need to question it until my unforeseen healer role came to light and was frowned upon by some parishioners, making me very uncomfortable with my beloved church family.

I am not intrusive, but I tried to tell some of them about my relationship with Jesus and the healing experiences. Most often they would change the subject, stop interacting, look over my shoulder as if I wasn't there, or excuse themselves.

It seemed as if many of them were closed up—desperate to hold onto their own belief systems—and weren't open to change without pastoral guidance. They needed to be told what they could or couldn't believe and didn't quite know what to accept of me. I could see in this small congregation a reflection of the collective consciousness in which humanity is afraid of change.

In the scientific community and elsewhere many have been conditioned to consider healing work as irrelevant and unreal unless it can be proven through rigorous, pragmatic controls according to specific tradition. And in my church family, some felt that claiming I had a healing gift was like intruding into sacred territory reserved only for Jesus and the Apostles.

I often wrote the man who, at that time, was pastor of my hometown church, to share my experiences of the many healings I was a part of in my travels. Once, when home between work assignments, I attended an adult Sunday school class, not knowing what to expect. The pastor asked me to tell the class about some of the healings I had written of in my letters. I was reluctant, but he prodded me on, from one story to another, saying, "Tell them about this . . ." and then . . . "Now tell them about this. . . ." Then, at the end of the class, he read from Mark 6: 1-6, the lesson for the day.

> He [Jesus] went away from there and came to His own country, and His disciples followed Him. And on the sabbath He began to teach in the synagogue; and many who heard him were astonished, saying, "Where did this man get all this? What is the wisdom given to Him? What mighty works are wrought by His hands! Is not this the carpenter, the son of Mary and the brother of James and Joses and Judas and Simon, and are not his sisters here with us!" And they took offense at Him. And Jesus said to them, "A prophet is not without honor, except in his own country, and among his own kin, and in his own house." And he could do no mighty work there, except that He laid His hands upon a few sick people and healed them. And He marveled because of their unbelief.

Either the pastor was telling me where I stood amongst my own people, or he was trying to introduce new concepts into their way of thinking, or both.

And as I write this, Jesus instills in my heart . . . *"I traveled far and wide and brought truths from the Far East and North Country back to my own land. My people had not been able to extend love to foreigners and, like your people, they were closed-up and would not open to the new wisdom offered, for it was foreign to them."*

* * *

Healing experiences and unfamiliar concepts also challenged my deeply-ingrained, learned, religious beliefs—in particular, the belief that one should not accept anything beyond the range of the traditional teachings and conventions of one's church. The work of modern-day healers was looked at with suspicion by many parishioners and pastors, yet I suddenly discovered I was a healer, witnessed healings happening before my eyes, and was changed. I soon realized I had to chose either my church family, which would have stymied my growth as a healer, or the living Christ in my heart. The thought of losing either was painful. The challenge lay in the choosing.

If I chose conventional, mainstream religion, I could settle back into my familiar, seemingly proper role, yet I knew that if I accepted my healing gift, even with its mystery, it would hasten the progression of my spiritual growth. I could not let this gift from God escape me.

And so, there was a flash of time when first there was a choice and then there was the choosing and then I was freed.

Somewhere it is written that "knowledge is taught but

understanding is a gift. To have both you must have freedom." Freedom includes unhindered empowerment to follow your inner guidance, and I could see that God was drawing me away from my hometown church and wanted me headed in a new direction.

It was interesting to me that, even though my hometown pastor had not called on me as a healer, those in other cities and states arranged for me to work with some of their parishioners in silent mission for the short time I was with them. Perhaps my being a stranger in their midst made it easier for them. Still, they were very careful, and it was most often secretive.

Though no longer able to fully embrace the beliefs and conventions of organized religion, I did attend various Christian churches, mostly Lutheran, on my three-month work assignments across the country, for I love communal worship.

It was comforting to pick up hymnals everywhere, with the same familiar hymns. However, I was becoming increasingly aware that the services and hymns lacked feminine gender. This patriarchal bias from the past, carried over into today's world, suddenly felt out of place to me— outdated—and raised even more questions in my mind.

In her book *The Dance of the Dissident Daughter,* Sue Monk Kidd[31] quoted from *A Doll's House*[32] (a Henrik Ibsen play), in which Nora announces she is leaving, to go away and discover her own life. I was curious about the play and had the local library borrow it for me. I found this

1879 social drama about the suppression of female individuality to be remarkably relevant for any era.

Nora's husband asks, "Are you not clear about your place in your own home? Have you not an infallible guide in questions like these? Have you not religion?"

Nora answers, "Oh, Torvald, I don't know properly what religion is . . . I know nothing but what our clergyman told me when I was confirmed. He explained that religion was this and that. When I get away from here and stand alone, I will look into that matter too. I will see whether what he taught me is true, or, at any rate, whether it is true for me."

Religion had muddled my mind too. This had not been a concern for me prior to becoming aware of my healing gift. Back then I was comfortable with a simple faith in God, keeping Jesus to myself, all while being oblivious to other religions, gender bias, church doctrine, and church politics. Now, I felt betrayed somehow, but didn't have the time or inclination to sort out who was right or wrong. I could only affirm, "I am a child of God."

As I write about and reflect with sadness on the difficulty some members of my church family had in accepting me as a healer, Jesus, ever-aware of my thoughts, opens my heart. I feel His indescribable presence within and it makes my heart glad.

"Mankind becomes what their perceptions in life teach them. Often, within the construct of self-limiting perceptions, they disregard what would help them grow

spiritually, because they cannot get past their learned traditions. Spiritual growth does not have restrictions. It is there for everyone.

"You receive from Spirit according to your openness for spiritual growth. The more you are open to and acknowledge Spirit, the more you receive. And the more you share your spirituality, the more you receive. For faith without action is useless."

How comforting and meaningful His words!

Then, suddenly, needing assurance with regard to my writings, I asked, "I hear you saying that the more we are open to Spirit and share our experiences, the more we receive. I can only assume then that spiritual experiences should not always be kept to oneself in sacred silence?"

"How will others learn if you do not share. Still, Brave Heart, you must remember each soul is on their own path, and all paths lead to God."

"Ah, Sweet Jesus. I need that reminder often."

This is all that was said at the time.

My relationship with Jesus is one of devotion, and in return, He provides me with spiritual realizations, companionship and love. Often I am simply aware of His presence in sweet silence.

Sometimes I feel as if I am saying too much. Or I wish I could be writing in the third person, as Saint Teresa of Avila often did,[33] so people would not know she was writing about herself. I would have preferred to keep things more to myself, within my own heart, but because Jesus has encouraged me to share my experiences, I put many of them in writing. I can only hope they will be of help to others on their spiritual path.

* * *

In the Bible, Saint Paul says that everyone has a gift to offer or role to play in the ongoing drama of life, to aid human existence.[34]

Although all of us have the potential to heal ourselves and others through God's love, those in whom this ability has manifested are spoken of as having the gift of healing.

However, the ego stands between us and God. Possessed of an ego, we see only separation where unity exists.[35] Through my experiences, I have discovered that a healer must be able to cast aside the ego—with all its illusions, limitations, and selfishness. When this takes place, a far greater reality comes into play. In this transformative purification, there is an emptying out of worldly desires and a filling up of God. Healing is then entrusted to God.

God is the source of the divine power and intelligence that work through one, but if one does not acknowledge God as the source, one soon begins to think of one's human self—the ego—as the source. One may become puffed-up with self-importance, more focused on the praise of others than on God, and one's spiritual gifts may slip away.

A healer should always pay attention to what the ego is stirring up, be it vanity, indifference to the needs of others, or arrogance.

In *Messages from Jesus - A Dialogue of Love,* Jesus said, *"Recognize that, when you are aware of the ego surfacing, it is showing you a situation you need to pay attention to and correct."*[36]

If a healer remains humble and loving, realizing that the life force, which heals, and the intelligence that guides us when we are truly inspired are not made or even understood by us, but are gifts from our Creator, ego cannot gain the upper hand, and through unselfish, loving service, the healer grows spiritually. Over time, the veils that obscure the full realization of God as infinite oneness, love and light are slowly lifted.

This is not only true for the healer, but it is also true for all of humanity.

There came a time when a pink angel made her presence known to me. I don't remember exactly when; it just seemed as if she had always been there.

I have never been able to intuit her name, for when I consider it, my mortal mind gets in the way with fanciful names that I think she must have, so I am never successful at getting her true name.

I think of her when I have need of her, and she is immediately there. It seems it is simply the thought of her image that triggers her appearance. Once she appears, I acknowledge her with love and address her as "My Pink Angel."

Often I have left her with people of all ages, in hospitals

and nursing homes. I would simply say to them, "Would you like to borrow my pink angel tonight? She will wrap you in her wings and hold you tight and comfort you." They were always eager to have her with them, and I gave her away over and over again.

On one of my assignments, I was asked to evaluate a ten-year-old girl, who had fallen out of a tree and broken both legs. She was in the intensive care unit, in a great deal of pain and fearful.

After doing the initial evaluation, I asked the parents if I could attempt to calm her using Healing Touch[37]. This is the name of a modality I had heard of but not felt moved to study. It was the only name I could think of, and at that time I didn't know how to explain what I did, because I had not studied anything about healing and was only going by what I was learning through my intuition, God and Jesus.

Today, I would have called it "energy work", a general term for any modality in which the healer uses healing energies to correct negativities or imbalances in the aura (the energy field that surrounds and interpenetrates one's body). Energy work can be used to induce relaxation response, alleviate pain, and accelerate the healing process.

With her parents' consent and as they stood by, I proceeded to silently pray and to smooth out her aura, and she quickly relaxed. Not only that, but I asked her if she would like to borrow my pink angel for the night. I told her that the pink angel would hold her and comfort her. She accepted.

The next day, my supervisor took me aside and said she had been called into a meeting with the hospital administrator, who told her that the parents had gone to their priest to ask if what I had done was acceptable. The priest was skeptical, so the parents had been in to meet with the administrator and voiced their misgivings about my treatment of their daughter.

The supervisor had stood up for me and told the administrator, and later the parents, that I do this as part of my treatment of patients and the effects are truly amazing. As a result of her intervention, I was allowed to treat the girl, but I had to promise not to use Healing Touch to heal her. However, I was given permission to use my healing gift wherever else I might feel moved to do so!

My supervisor, initially, had also been skeptical. As I sat at my hand-therapy desk, treating out-patient after out-patient, I could feel her watching me closely from across the room, where the door of her office was always left open, and she was able to visually take in the whole therapy room.

She watched me when patients came to me with excruciating pain, reluctant to be touched, only to have their pain decreased and their fears calmed very quickly through the healing energy. For that is what I felt each time—a tremendous energy coming from my hands and heart. And further, she realized before long that the patients gained greater range of motion and healed faster than the norm.

My supervisor was able to watch me enough to gain confidence in my healing work and saw value in it, thus she was able to stand up for me in regard to the little girl, her parents and the hospital administrator.

For a brief period, after the incident with the little girl, nothing seemed to be happening in my healing work. Discouraged, I called the pastor of the church I was attending while on this assignment. He listened but did not comment. I called a friend. Same thing; no comment. I talked to Jesus. He didn't respond either. I thought I might have done something to displease God and my healing gift had been taken away.

The next day at work, the first hand patient said, "Since you have been doing this, I don't have pain anymore." The second hand patient said, "Since you have been doing this, I can sleep nights now." The third hand patient said, "Since you have been doing this, I can handle this now."

Suddenly, I realized that God was teaching me an important lesson, that there is more to healing than the physical, that healing encompasses body, mind and soul! This was something I needed to know, for I was new to healing and thought of it only in terms of physical changes.

Also, I realized that a healer does not tell God what to do and should have no attachment to outcome.[38]

One day, a skeptical physical therapist, who worked in the same large therapy room as I did, came over and threw himself across my desk, arms spread out, and said, "Tell me where my pain is and what to do about it!" I laughed at him and without hesitation said, "There is nothing wrong with you except that you have a major headache." I grabbed the pain, as if I were grasping something from thin air, and held it in my tightened fist. I said to him, "Here is your pain," and I tossed it away. His headache was gone. He believed in my work after that.

I was fearless with my healing gift. If confronted by a skeptic, I was able to say the right things in the moment, or sensed when to back off so as not to be intrusive.

In another setting, I treated an eighteen-year-old male, who had been rear-ended in an accident and left with paralysis and other problems. It was made clear to me that he did not want me treating him. He wanted one of the young therapists.

Reluctantly, he worked with me. Soon, he became fascinated by my manner of treatment, for I introduced healing to him. I had absolutely no doubt that healing energy would work for him.

One day he said to me, "I told my grandmother about you, and she wants to meet you." Another day when I went in to treat him, his room was full of relatives. I walked in to start my work, but my feet took me to a very elderly woman. I walked up to her, without introduction, for I knew she was his grandmother. I put my arms around her and, with nothing said, we exchanged a profound energy that melded us together as if we were long-lost friends. I knew she was a healer.

This patient complained to the nursing staff, his doctor, and myself about a terrible, recurring stomach-ache, so severe he didn't want to follow through with his treatment. I used healing energy on him, and the pain was gone.

Soon after, we were in the large therapy room, where I was having him do some gross motor activity, and his doctor came in, sat down on the huge, raised mat and said, "You are my star patient. You are getting well so fast it is unbelievable." And then, "So what happened to that stomach pain you were complaining about?" The patient turned, pointed at me and said, "Well, ever since she has been doing healing work on me, I haven't had any pain and I'm doing really well." The doctor turned to me and asked, "So what kind of healing work do you do?" I felt one of those moments come on when I wanted to leave for fear of losing my job. I stood and quickly said, "It is called Healing Touch, but I have to be excused to check on another patient." I knew nothing at the time about Healing Touch, for I had not studied it.

As I quickly left, I wished I had not been so hasty in my retreat, for the doctor had a look on his face that has haunted me ever since, seemingly telling me he wanted to hear more and I didn't take the time.

Twice before, I had tried ignoring God or Jesus, after specific directives, and missed opportunities to serve. It didn't go well. Both times I felt a deep sense of discomfort and regret. I also felt I missed out on some wonderful experience by not following what I knew deep inside to be guidance from Spirit.

After two years of not reading or studying anything about healing, I was suddenly compelled to start studying different healing modalities. I could not ignore the urging.

I now have many certificates from classes I attended and use terminology and specific healing modalities when moved to do so. However, the important thing I learned is that my intuition, and guidance from Jesus and Spirit is all I truly need.

With studying behind me—and, then again, learning never ends—and without being overly assertive, I continued to strive to increase awareness among medical personnel in hospitals and facilities where I worked of how healers can fit into the medical model.

Do I understand how healing takes place? I don't feel I need to. I simply do what I am moved to do. How do I know it is God or Jesus directing me? Through their presence as love, I let go of ego and am filled with love, which overflows with feelings of bliss into effortless expressions of healing.

While working in a hospital in New Mexico, I met a distinguished, kind-hearted man. We started dating, and eventually married. I thought this was it, forever, a companion who understood my healing role. We took an apartment in a city near my next assignment. All was well until the day came when our values clashed.

In my new placement, I was soon offered a supervisory position, full time, for an impressive amount of money. I decided to think about it. At about the same time, I inherited a hand trauma client from an occupational therapist who was leaving her job. I soon realized I should discharge him because he had plateaued after months of treatment. I offered him healing, and he accepted. Overnight, he was able to make a fist and had a grip strength of twenty pounds. Previously, he had been unable to do either. I discharged him shortly thereafter and gave him a home exercise program to strengthen his grip further and improve his fine motor skills.

Some time later, the supervisor of the therapy department called the occupational therapists into a meeting, along with administration and some others I didn't know. The supervisor stood and said to me, "We understand you healed Mr. . . . . We can't have that here. We have to keep our doctors happy and this doctor is not happy with this situation. We have a hard time getting doctors to come here and we have to go with what they want. No more healing!

Amazed, I stood up and said, "No problem, it won't

happen again. I would like to be excused; I have clients waiting." They excused me and I left. After I left, they asked the other OT's how they would feel about someone like me supervising them. They stood up for me and said that I was never intrusive with patients and staff.

When I told my new husband what had happened and that I could not take the job offer because I could not envision permanently working in a hospital that did not allow healing, he began to shout at me incessantly for three days. "How could you turn down such a lucrative position just because you couldn't do your thing?" Shades of Dave passed through me.

On top of that, we had transplanted a small bush in our yard, which then dried up, lost its leaves, became brittle and appeared to be dead. We had tried everything we could think of to keep it going. I voiced the fact that I was upset about losing it. He sarcastically said to me, "Why don't you do your thing on that bush?" That was an amazing statement coming from a husband who suddenly didn't like what I was doing—even more amazing because I had never thought of this. Since I was at that point in my life where I had chosen not to study healing, I did not know plants had auras and it never occurred to me they could be healed.

I sent loving, healing energy into the plant, and overnight, it had all new buds and leaves on it. My husband was so shocked and uncomfortable with the whole situation that we divorced within days.

"Once again, don't overlook how God teaches us lessons.

Many lessons were taught here. Through your husband you were made aware that plants have auras. You did not deny your gift, and from this, you came to the realization that you no longer needed someone with you in your life."

As I approached the end of that assignment, after three years of three-month work settings, I suddenly felt compelled to quit traveling and go back to Michigan. There was a peaceful knowing that I did not need to be married. I felt whole—with no resentment toward that husband—free, in charge, and true to myself.

I phoned an agency that employs traveling therapists, asked if they had anything in Michigan, and they said, "Yes, we have a setting in Manistee, Michigan." Manistee was my hometown. I was being called back home!

THE DESERT

The wind wakes me
to watch the blue-green haze of juniper
meeting the face of the sun.

I listen to the sand
singing with the wind,
and the desert marigolds shiver
when the wind whistles over.

It is a fine morning,
for the wind tells me it is.
And it tells me
where it was before,
where it blew the clouds,
whether it will rain,
and whither I go.

Driving into Michigan, I was struck by the brightness of everything; the sky seemed bluer and the grass greener than I had remembered. Everything had a brilliance, with light outlining it. I felt welcomed by everything in view. It felt right to be in Michigan again.

In my hometown there were familiar faces. The organist at the church I grew up in had quit and I was offered the job—the same job I had quit just prior to leaving Michigan for the three years on the road as a traveling therapist. I almost felt as if I had never left, but I wasn't that person anymore. I was changed.

In my heart, I knew this was temporary and that I would not be there long. Contemplating my future, I asked, "What next Lord?" and prayed for time off.

Thinking back on it now, I realize God wanted me home for the trial and blessings to come.

Chapter Eight

An Awakening

O . . . my soul sings
sweet songs . . .
the anthems of my life.

Singing stills my soul
and sweeps all else away.

My eyes flew open, from out of the depths of a deep, lovely slumber, as the 1998 New Year's morning began to dawn. Something strange was happening to me. My pelvic floor clamped shut, containing within me a powerful, pulsating, flowing energy, which spread up my spine, out into my limbs, and into my head as if I were a vessel to be filled, then emptied, then filled and emptied, again and again.

This was different, somehow, from other energies I would sometimes feel. Usually there was a warm or cold energy, invading vertebrae and searching every pore. Now I could only give myself up to the wonder of the all-encompassing, fierce, fiery invasion, as if it were cleansing me to start the New Year fresh. Tears of joy flowed from my eyes. Every energy-filled breath seemed to build upon each preceding breath.

In surrendering to its intensity, there was no fear, just an all-pervading, blissful calm, and I went where physical sound does not exist and time is unknown. . . .

Ah, Holy Jesus, peacefulness surrounds me;
nothing in the silence tells me I am weeping.
Oh, Holy Jesus, comforter forever,
enter in my being.

When I returned to normal consciousness, I sensed the energy slowly subsiding, draining out from every part of me, and as it left, I realized it was taking more than I had to give. In its absence, I could barely lift my left arm and leg and had a difficult time sitting up. Still . . . I felt peaceful, unafraid.

My daughter, Lorelei, and granddaughter, Allysha, had celebrated New Year's Eve with me in the comfort of my home. They were still sound asleep, elsewhere in the house. I called out and my daughter came quickly. I told her to drive me to the hospital because I thought I might be having a stroke. I didn't know how else to explain it. My daughter did not drive at the time, but I felt sure she could get me to the hospital faster than if I waited for an ambulance.

With her help, I sat on the top step of the stairway and

managed to semi-slide downstairs; then she helped me into the car. While she drove us to the hospital, I urged her on, even telling her to go through a red light. I didn't want to waste any time, as I realized that I was losing more and more function.

By the time we got to the hospital, I could barely lift my left arm. It would fall any which way, at my side or across my face. I tested it often, each time measuring the difference in my ability to lift my arm at all. It was almost fun, a test of self-mastery. My strength would quickly give out. I felt imbalanced throughout my whole body. Even my cognition was impaired.

Still, there wasn't any fear, only a silence within me. There was no questioning, no remorse and no concern about death, just a feeling of contentment, as I felt Jesus' presence only a breath away.

The decrease in function finally leveled off after I had been in the hospital several hours. I was left with extreme overall weakness and left-sided paralysis of the upper and lower extremities, only to next be filled up with pain . . . painful headache and pains in my legs. I prayed for healing.

I was put in a hospital room with a roommate. She was elderly, very ill, and couldn't quit coughing. As I lay there, I sent love to her and prayed for her long into her restless night. A loving presence filled the room, as I imagined my beloved pink angel fanning soft wings over her body, healing her; and I too, surrendered to sleep within my pink angel's healing grace.

My roommate went home the next day. Then I had the room to myself.

And today, as I write about this experience and read it back to myself, I feel Jesus' presence within my heart.

Jesus whispers, *"Blessed are those who, in acts of love, endeavor to change the suffering of others while paying no regard to their own personal suffering. They, too, change in a twinkling of an eye."*

"Ah Sweet Jesus, how beautiful your words. It is never a difficult choice. Can I stand by and do nothing while others suffer?"

"You did not choose to come to earth for illusive nothings."

The blissful warmth of Jesus' love flows through me like waves of warm, gentle wind, and I smile within.

And, with that, Jesus faded away into a crystal mist.

The diagnosis given was "stroke." But they couldn't find a cause except for an increase in the megahertz of brain activity.

I was suddenly thrown into a world of therapy. Doctors, nurses, concerned family and friends, all were ever-full of restless abstractions of what they thought was best for me. And all the while, a peaceful feeling embraced me.

Ah, Holy Spirit, powerful Your presence—
cleansing and renewing,
searching deep within me.

O Holy Spirit, bathe me with Your glory.
All my days I praise Thee.

Just before this powerful surge of energy with its debilitating consequences, I had asked God to give me time off. I wanted to meditate on these questions: "What next?" and "Where do I go from here?" Now I had plenty of time off, just what I had asked for. An enforced rest is probably the only way I would have taken the time. I looked at my circumstances as a gift, so I could meditate—to prepare myself for what was to come—then take whatever journey was asked of me.

Jesus has often repeated, *"Manifestation comes with sound intentions."*

At every moment of our lives, we are on the threshold of potential, new journeys, or change, which if pursued will lead to personal and spiritual growth. There is always a starting point, a catalyst that can shift your life in an instant if you let it. It might be a thought that sparks an effort on your part to do the right thing, a spiritual insight, a tragedy, or a heartfelt affirmation. In my case, I had asked for time off, and my prayer was granted. And I was about to discover, in what had happened, a far greater blessing than what I had asked for.

Although we may ask for change, the opportunity is often gone with the wind if we do not intuitively recognize the purpose of whatever has manifested for us and run free with it, even if society might find this outrageous.

With decreased cognition, strength and coordination, but slowly improving ambulation and use of my left arm, I was finally able to go home from the hospital.

I refused to have anyone stay with me. I thought I would be fine on my own, but my cognition was poor for many things, including decision making. My first morning home, I decided to make myself some breakfast. I took an egg out of the refrigerator and studied it for a while. For a second I was unable to determine how to get into it. Then I remembered to crack it.

It was the same with my music. Prior to my New Year's Day experience, I had sung in a performance of the "Messiah" at the Ramsdell Theater and accompanied our church choir on the organ in a cantata for Christmas. But now, even music I had played on the piano for many years was unfamiliar to me. I began to play it slowly—one finger at a time, one measure at a time—painstakingly relearning lost skills.

Family and friends came to help me during the day, bringing more food than I knew what to do with. I felt as if I were a part of a huge event, and I was. I could only accept what had already taken place, not knowing what was to come. Jesus was with me, as always, constantly encouraging me.

Soon after I came home from the hospital, a director of music for the Ramsdell Theater, Jim Bond, came over, not aware that I had just been hospitalized. He came to offer me the alto solo in St. John's Passion, to be sung for Easter.

I had always wanted a lead role in one of Bach's musical works. What more wondrous way is there to honor Jesus than with singing?

I had sung on the radio as a seven year old. I had played female lead parts in thirteen musicals at the historic Ramsdell Theater and a local college. I sang in the Messiah when it was offered. And I loved Bach's music.

I told Jim I couldn't do it, hiding my deep disappointment. After he left, I knew I had to release the desire of ever performing solo parts in St. John's Passion or any other great work, for I couldn't even play the simple music waiting on my piano! I did not want to hold onto this desire. In flowing tears I looked out the window upon my beloved river and willed myself to let it go, not by giving up ambition but simply by not clinging to the desire as a part of myself any longer. Slowly it flowed out from me, as surely as the river flows.

The river rushes by like life in a hurry.
Earth weighs me down.
With effort, I move on.

The Manistee River symbolized many things to me. Ever-flowing—never letting up, always there—the river was a constant reminder to me not to give up. There were times when I was so at one with the river I felt I could walk on it.

Sometimes the wind and rolling water awakened hidden emotions from deep within me. Other times, the water barely moved and lulled me into quiet meditation.

The river is fringed with a river-walk from the east of town to Lake Michigan, and it holds in its keep sea gulls and river traffic, including huge lower-laker ships and fishermen, with sounds and activities of life from which I took strength. The river flows two-hundred miles, from its source into Lake Michigan, a stone's throw from my home.

Peace, like the river, and solitude led me to greater awareness of my inner identity. Feeling ever-closer to God, I finally had reached a time in my life wherein I was content with myself and being alone. A liberating feeling. Something to celebrate, and I did.

One of the entries in my journal went thus:

The full moon is sitting on the horizon of the great lake, where the sun usually sets, awaiting its own descension. Moonlight is lighting up the fringes of the spaced-out cirrus clouds and, in violet reflection, dances amidst the rolling current on the river just outside my window. The panoramic sky changes moment by moment.

In joyous thoughts, I dance on the river, in the light of the violet moon, so deep into meditation that my body disappears. And I am aware of merging with the moonlit, violet reflections dancing upon the river.

Seems like this is all I really want to do lately. Becoming a monastic sounds inviting.

Some days I had more strength and some days less. I constantly had to challenge my endurance to increase my strength, and my mind to increase my cognition. Gradually, there were more good days than bad days.

And there was therapy. On the treadmill, I would close my eyes, hang on with one hand for balance, since my vestibular system wasn't perfect yet, and swing the other arm. I experienced excruciating headache and pain in my legs, and my endurance for the sustained exercise was very poor. I could only do less than a quarter mile, walking slowly.

Then one day, I remembered a favorite saying of mine.

Mindfulness is:
When you are doing something,
focus only on that.

So, instead of remaining separate from the pain, I meditated on the pain. I entered the pain, calling on Jesus: "Jesus . . . Jesus . . . Jesus. . . . " I became so at one with the pain and Jesus that I lost body consciousness. I walked and walked, over a mile, without pain, before being stopped by the therapist. My heart rate had not increased!

My therapist told me I had to quit meditating during therapy since, without the increase in heart rate, it would not benefit my cardiovascular system.

The doctor continued to say that the "stroke" was caused by increased megahertz of activity in the brain. Still nothing showed up on the MRI or EEG except that my brain was functioning way above the norm, and there was no indication of any cardiovascular problem.

Three years later, Jesus told me, *"You did not have a stroke. You had an awakening."*

I replied, "I had many symptoms of a stroke, including partial paralysis. Yet, they couldn't find a cause, except for an increase in megahertz of brain activity."

Later on, Jesus spoke of it as a "kundalini" awakening.[39] At the time it happened, I had no idea of what an awakening was, much less, a kundalini awakening. However, energy surges were not new to me. I had experienced them since early childhood, but didn't give them much mind. I never dreamed an energy surge could be so powerful and totally encompassing as to leave one impaired.

Following that major awakening, there was a definite change in my spiritual self. My cognition for practical things had been impaired, but my awareness of spiritual things had been further enhanced. Often, my mind felt open and free, rather than impaired, as if I were of a different mind, the mind of my soul. Ever-deeper communion and oneness with Spirit and nature filled me, increased visionary insight was given to me, and I began to write poetry describing the blissful feelings, visions, and realizations I was having.

It was as if all my life I was being made ready for this kundalini awakening. All the poetry interspersed in my books came to me after this event, as if preparing me to be a writer.

I lived alone, back then, in the quiet simplicity of my riverside home.

One bright morning I left open the door to the deck outside my bedroom upstairs. Soon large flies began to invade my healing room downstairs where I was writing. I was being bombarded by them. I was so intent on what I was doing that I just kept swishing them away. Finally, I stopped and, with reverent heart talk to their guiding intelligence, asked to have them gather on the screen doors and, when I was done, I would let them out.

Silence prevailed, and I actually forgot about them. When I was finished with my writing, I had to go past the front door and there, gathered on the screen, were a good twenty flies waiting. I let them out, then went to the back door and let that gathering out, then closed the upstairs slider.

One day I went outside to stain the railing on my deck, which is about thirty feet long. There were spider webs and insects all along its length. I walked down each side, again respectfully requesting that the little insect critters move off the railing, as I was about to stain it, and said that, when I was finished and the odor was gone, it would be safe to come back.

I never ran into a single insect while doing the staining, and they did come back after a few days.

I think, when used in a consciousness of oneness, heart talk emanates into a universal language that all creatures including humans have the innate potential to understand.

My days were filled with rehabilitation, meditation, healing, and rest. I felt that this was what I was supposed to be doing. I would put a blanket in the dryer to warm it, unplug the phone, lock the doors, light incense and candles, safe within their own containers, drop essential oil into the hot wax, put on some meditative music, and lie down on my healing table, where so many others had come for healing. Now it was my turn. I would cover myself with the warmed blanket and, while the music played its lilting sounds within the sacred atmosphere, I would praise God.

The air in the healing room would become highly energized; you could smell the sweetness of it. The sounds of my breath and the beat of my heart would slow in peaceful harmony.

Before my awakening, when others would come for healing, I would say a prayer for guidance. Most often, I would be moved to brush and cleanse their auras of impurities, which required arm movement. But now, I didn't have the physical strength to raise my arms for long, so I called upon Jesus, my spirit friends and my pink angel to take over for me, and they were there.

All waves of thought would subside, as I surrendered my old self and my pink angel fanned me with her soft, downy, healing wings, in the presence of Jesus and my spirit friends. Blissful, healing energies would spread through me. Sometimes tears would flow from me, as if they were a gift, freeing something within that was no longer needed . . . an inner transformation. And I would often sleep in this sacred space, all night until early dawn, only to start all over again. And I slowly healed.

Chapter Nine

A Different Way of Being

A PRAYER FOR OUR ENEMIES

O poor and hungry of the world,
Unkindly treated and oppressed,
Who, thus, despise the fortunate;
With love and light may you be blessed.

And you who counsel them with lies,
Who—filled with anger, hate and spite—
Do urge them on to kill;
We send you love and light.

May mercy and forgiveness rule,
For only love can end the violence and fear
That all on earth have helped create
In distant past and near.

Though mortal enemies now cause us pain,
We've done the same to others in lives past.
Help us, O God—by seeing Thee in all—
To end the dismal cycle, else it last.

Amen

— George Johnston

I wondered, as I had many times after my awakening, if the energies that expanded my brain activity to higher dimensions of wakefulness might also have altered my DNA, and if this could improve my health.

I regarded my thoughts about DNA as mere whimsy, but then Jesus, within my heart, omnipresent . . . disclosed . . .

"Anyone who increasingly responds to life with love and compassion has positive change in their DNA structure."

I asked,   "Love changes our genetics?"

"With love. . . your DNA, in enhanced response, affects you in all aspects of life on all levels. It is a reciprocal relationship. In expressing good or bad habits in all of your thoughts and activities of life, you in turn receive wellness or afflictions in body, mind and spirit. Your DNA is affected by all that you do and think. Love or lack of it defines your being.

"God is love, and you are an expression of God. Remember to remember the love that you are."

"Does that make us all God?"

"God, the Highest Good, is wholly you and everyone else. However, you are not wholly God, for you are but an expression of God's love, as love is His likeness, and God created you in His likeness. Your Highest Good is your God-self, your likeness in God.

"Until you can realize and grow in the love that you are, your awareness will be contained within the dualistic realm. Ah . . . if each person could live in love, they would

realize that Heaven on Earth is a breath away, and dualistic perceptions would begin to fall to the wayside, as snow falling quietly to the ground.

"Brave Heart, you have chosen to give of yourself, as love and compassion, to others. Your mission has barely begun."

Suddenly I felt a seriousness within my heart, and I sensed the same seriousness in Jesus' face. He stopped and grew quiet. I wanted to reach up and touch His face. But I waited—subdued by His expression—then, slowly, as if He wanted to make sure His words were understood correctly, He said,

"All that I say, I say for all mankind. Think about a time when you felt deep love toward someone. . . . Stop a moment and think about how it felt. . . . That very act of giving love was a giving of your self as love. . . . In that moment, you opened your heart and experienced the love that you are . . . and, within that giving, loving feeling . . . even if for only a moment . . . you became at one with another. . . .You experienced heaven on earth.

"Imbibe your self as love—within the sick and the vengeful . . . the earth . . . the air—with healing, peaceful thoughts. For your whole world needs love and peace.

"And, when you learn to love yourself, you will come to know yourself as love . . . and healing happens even for you . . . within your whole being as body, mind and spirit."

And now, several years after this beautiful communion with Jesus, while rereading His loving words, they cause me to close in upon myself. Holding myself in a hug, I try to imagine loving myself. Waiting, in my self-embrace, I feel nothing. I bend over to rest my head on my desk, still embracing myself. Still nothing. A deep breath seems to take over and I let out a long sigh, finally able to let go of trying so hard.

Slowly, on an intake of breath, I feel the warmth of unconditional love—flowing like a river—spreading everywhere within me. And I bathe a while in the depth of this bliss bath of love.

Suddenly, in a vision, I see terrorists everywhere, and I ask Jesus for protection as I merge into them. We cannot tell each other apart. There is no fear, no sorrow, and no judgment. I feel only love, and in the vision, we are enveloped in love and changed, terrorists and me alike. And time passes, gently. . . .

Then, I am made aware of Jesus' comforting presence. He has such a silence about him that I suddenly realize I cannot hear Him breathing and can't remember if I ever have.

He slowly whispers, with great feeling, so I cannot miss the significance of what He is saying, *"I do not speak of love in complex, dualistic terms. I speak only of simple, unadulterated, non-dual love. Everyone has this pure love within, none other in my eyes. Love is God and God is Love.*

"Your world needs this love revealed. I cannot express in human terms how important it is at this time, for you could not tolerate its immensity. Just remember . . . with love, nothing is impossible."

I have to stop here. It is more than I can bear, to hear Jesus so adamantly displaying His concern in an emotional whisper. It is more powerful than if He shouted.

Suddenly I recall a recent show I saw on television. A black man was telling about his youth when he had no one to look up to. He lived in poverty and violence here in the United States. He didn't know of much else. He didn't know about God, heros, love, or goodness until he was imprisoned. It was there, after several years had passed, that he reached out and became more than he had ever hoped to be, eventually leaving prison and becoming a successful chef in a prestigious restaurant.

Another memory flashes in my mind, of a documentary about a tribe of South American natives who lived in a way they thought was normal: warring on their neighbors and wiping out whole villages. Love was revealed to them through missionaries.

Then I see another vision. I see young men being coerced into joining terrorist groups, unable to say no. I see their family members in jeopardy or killed for trying to do what is right.

I can't seem to bring myself to ask the questions that are forming in my mind. So I can only quiet myself and let the warmth of love envelope me, fill me. With a smile, I throw the love, as if it were a blanket, to fall gently upon all who do not know of love—those at war within themselves and those caught up in war against each other.

* * *

SHOWER OF LOVE

Imagine loving warmth enveloping you . . .
forming you into a vessel to be filled. . . .
Love pours into you. . . .
Healing pours into you. . . .
Divine Peace pours into you. . . .
Overflowing. . . .

Then, in a moment you choose,
throw open your arms and,
as a gentle shower of love,
rain forth goodness . . .
over the earth . . .
over friend and foe
or situation. . . .

* * *

I was recuperating nicely, when a friend said to me, "You should go to the Song of the Morning Retreat."[40] An immediate feeling of needing to go there came over me, moved me. I felt a rush of energy as Jesus came to my side urging me to ask more questions about the Retreat. And I did.

Chapter Ten

Song of the Morning

Oh . . . the footsteps of the Master—
No far stretch in His slow stride—
Draw me close to follow after,
Draw me safely to His side.

Deep within me, fire glows,
And when there is pause to praise,
I write the words, which simply flow,
Onto the hallowed page.

In the autumn of my life and in recuperation from the effects of the unannounced awakening so intense that I became disabled, I journey to Song of the Morning Retreat to rest for a while. I had encountered many setbacks in my efforts to make arrangements to come to the Retreat. It was only in surrendering to the process that I was finally able to come.

At the very entrance to Song of the Morning, I stop my car, unable to proceed. Held at bay by energy which takes my breath away, my mind is momentarily blank, as if it is being freed of all that is ephemeral and returns to dust. Then breath returns and fills me with sweet energies.

I open the car windows to more fully take in the wintry scene, and as I inhale, an icy blast of wind enters my very being, triggering a rolling surge of energy up my spine. It seems careful in its progression, or am I controlling it? . . . I can't say which. Then I simply "am" for a time.

How can anyone explain ecstatic bliss, or rapture? There are no words.

Suddenly, just as quickly as it came, it is over. Peace reigns within me as I slowly resume my pilgrimage.

The unblemished air feels sliced by my intrusion, as I slowly drive into a welcoming, brilliant, white castle of ice and snow, escorted by dancing, shimmering snow crystals. I joyfully travel . . . amidst sunbeams, over snow, on snow, on snow . . . under azure sky and a canopy of icy, diamond-laden branches, which form a portal into which I am drawn.

Why does this flawless diadem of beauty, far from imagined, differ from the beauteous snow dreams I just drove through to get here? Why am I having this experience, this awareness? The answer can only be found in the other seeing, the one that, since my awakening, shows me things beyond the veil, drawing me to the other side of delusion.

I want the journey to last forever. I am in no hurry. I find joy and strength in this beautiful passage to the rest of my life, and I haven't even arrived yet.

I come to a lake of sparkling ice . . . with billows of snow dancing gaily upon its surface. The abrupt change from the embracing, ice-gemmed branches overhead to an expanse of ice and mirrored sky takes my breath away.

A poem comes to mind—one that I had written before coming here . . . possibly for this moment.

THE ICY GLASS

Stepping upon the icy glass . . .
looking down into the mirror,
I see myself in winter white,
layered, layered gossamer.

It floats upon my head and crown
and trails down to wrap around
my eyes and forehead so I can see . . .
the softness whispering into me.

Tendrils of the gossamer
fall, layered soft, upon my heart,
and gently, from the depths within,
move me to dance and let love in.

Gossamer, upon gossamer . . .
snow on snow on snow,
wraps my waist and, from within,
is lighting up my soul.

Then, without-within,
gossamer begins to wind . . .
round and round then up my spine,
with feelings of sheer ecstasy,
from base to crown and into air,
floating out as waves of light . . .
circling all with gossamer.

I look up from the mirrored ice,
refreshed and newly energized,
and realized . . .
then walk upon the icy glass.

The road does not end here, but continues over a small dam, holding the lake at bay, allowing just so much rushing water to flow from beneath the lake's icy crystal coat; and upon the dam, I stop.

"Ah, Sweet Jesus," I exclaim, "What a beautiful reprieve you have led me to . . . this miraculous repose of nature's glorious power."

I step out of the warmth of my car, into the cold wind, to look down into the watery overflow from the dam. Suddenly, from out of me pours a rush of my mind's ever-flowing thoughts, loosened by the fierce wind to spill into the booming waterfall. Deep breaths stay a bubbling cry, triggered from deep inside me, for only so long, then tears pour forth over the dam into the roaring water. I feel it reach into the recesses of my being, as healing releases pour forth until they leave me near empty.

Refreshed, I feel as if I have been reborn or won something—I'm not sure what. "Home at last," my superconscious mind screams in my semi-muffled ears. Not ready to truly listen, I can only tell a fresh start, a baptism. That much I can do.

Arriving at destiny's door, with no expectations and wanting nothing, I am directed to the lodge, where I unpack. Then, with no thought, I lie down upon the bed, letting my mind rest in comfort. I fall asleep like a child— asleep in ease.

Summoned to a far geodome for hatha yoga, I leave my car behind and walk. I thought I had to sign up for a class in order to come here. I know nothing about yoga.

I pace myself, stopping now and then to sit upon the cold snow sparkles to gather strength. Such freedom I find in the absence of my beloved caregivers. Such peace I find in not rushing.

I lie back upon the inviting snow and gaze longingly up into the sky, as dancing sparks rain down from out of the depths of the blue, and all the while I cry and laugh aloud and dance within. Uninhibited in my solitude, I am free to lose myself in joy, renew myself, and find myself, over and over again. Amused and ever-joyful am I at the play of my own mind.

Ah . . . the ecstasy of pain transforming into laughter, air becoming the breath of God, myself becoming the snow I lie upon, becoming the sky and river that greet my eyes. Ah . . . the paradox: the dualistic and nondualistic forces expressing, shape-shifting from oneness to duality and back again.

I take Jesus' offered hand as He helps me up and urges me on, then I enter the domed place. I doff my wintry fluff down to comfortable attire, and the instructor, sensing my need, tells me to just lie down, so I quietly join the yogis on the floor. I'm exhausted, as predicted by my caregivers, from these freedoms I took before my time.

I lie down and say a prayer for strength, then feel a breath upon my face, for my pink angel is there, fanning me with wings of healing grace. When called upon or needs arise she brushes me with love and heals my body and soothes my mind and soul.

Then I smell roses. I breathe the fragrance into the depths of my being. I can even taste it, and the rose fragrance fills me . . . lingering on and on, while sunrays beam down through a skylight star. No fear have I for such blissful energies . . . for gifts such as these.

I ease into sleep . . . healing in the warmth of my pink angel's love, covered by sunrays under the skylight star, under a fragrant rose blanket, in the company of yogis, in the midst of life as it goes on. And time stands still while I gain needed strength in peaceful slumber.

Summoned at mealtime, I silently don my winter clothes and make my way to the dining hall . . . another challenge; this time, uphill and the going slow. Again I often stop to become the snow and drink of its strength. Still, I do not feel rushed, as I slowly walk one step at a time, one foot before the other, as if this were something wonderful to do, and it is . . . a far cry from the paralysis of recent time.

While in concentrated meditation on my every step, Jesus is walking beside me, prodding me on as I climb, leading me to where I am to go. Overjoyed by such freedom, away from those who love me so, I play in this nurturing and sacred space, alone in God, with Jesus at my side.

I am late again, but I had learned rushing cannot be the way for me. I sit amidst the dining yogis, in a daze, with food before me, hunger vanished. Then noticing a bubbling cry, I quickly leave the food and yogis gathered there. With stayed sighs, I don my wintry attire once more and slowly make my way, further still, up the hill to the lodge, with lamenting cries, releasing . . . I know not what. I pause to rest and let my emotions spill until they are no more, and I am left with peace and inner strength.

Oh, the blessed lodge . . . provider of nurturing space . . . welcomes me with open arms. I sleep the evening and night away and dream of chanting such as I had never heard. Sacred words play on and on within my dreamy world, as safe lie I within this healing lodge. Ah . . . blissful dreams, wherein the dark is one with light, holding truths untold in delusional time!

And, in the morning, in the new day's sun, I enter the center room of the lodge and find myself before a stonework fireplace, and upon the mantle is a shrine with pictured saintly ones. With awe I lie upon the floor, amidst eclectic décor, under the gaze of the saintly ones, while time is undefined . . . and I feel as only a breath from God. Blanketed with love, I sleep again, unaware of delusion, and dream as one with them.

Upon waking, I am drawn to a picture on the mantle, bigger than the rest, of a saintly one smiling down upon me. I stand and look closely at him. I wander to and fro, and his gaze follows me. "Ah, most kind and gentle friend, I'm told you are Yogananda," I say, as I continue to walk slowly back and forth within the room. His steady gaze follows me. Then I settle upon the floor in quiet surrender, and in my meditation faintly hear . . . "Home at last. . . ."

I am alone in the lovely lodge, as if it were all for me. But in the evening, the yogis come to meditate. The dream of chanting such as I had never heard replays in real time, as they sing those same dreamed, mesmerizing chants.

I am comforted to hear their prayers, to saints and sages everywhere, and to see Sweet Jesus, Mother Mary, and my new friend among the pictured saintly ones upon the stonework altar shrine. And God, as love, is within my heart, binding us all together in present time.

The instrumental drones play on and on and on, as chanting fills the air. With arms upraised, my hands and fingers dance, as if in sign to those unseen, as if I were of the northern lights, flowing in the oneness of all there seems. Overcome by the rhythmic chants, with orchestrated breath I dance, on and on in trance. My vapor, luminescent whim, ribbon like, freely swims beyond the earthbound atmosphere.

Suddenly, the air is quieted of song . . . as I sit within this meditative space and hear, within my soul, the chanting still going on and on. And the words become mantras; and my fingers, mudras. Then I am moved to silently pray:

"Oh God,
I speak to Thee from mind and heart.
Over and over You come to me,
in the busiest time of day and in the dark.

Where am I to go,
now that You have expanded my senses
and left me pained,
while in joy I walk?

Is my presence here ordained?

Oh, Beloved God, I give myself to You;
I am Yours.
Wherever You lead,
I will follow. "

Silent songs of thankfulness and praise flow from me, in language I cannot explain, while energies arise from within, awakening me ever further to all that is and will be. I become the songs of prayer and lose all sense of separation from God.

The days and I move slowly on, and I am challenged only by wintry journeys as far as the dining hall. I could have stayed forever in this lovely, wintry haven, safely anchored in God's grace, under the watchful care of Yogananda and Jesus, free from delusion. Such leisure within our duality is rare. Yet, my final hours in this refuge arrive as I go outside very early one morning to welcome the morning air and nature.

As I observe the rising sun, a gentle, crystal spread of fire enters within me a knowing . . . a blunt reality that the time has come to leave, with the promise of sweet morning strength to see me through the readmittance into delusion and to reconstruct what some call reality, the realm of action, in which silence and peace are hidden until found.

Reluctantly bidding farewell to this wintry garden of God . . . this Song of the Morning . . . I leave as slowly as I arrived.

Suddenly, I feel as if a magnet is drawing me back. I stop the car. All is still, as in a tug of war where both sides are even and I am in the middle. Then something seems to say to me, "Away with you for now," and swiftly I am freed to drive on, as if I am being propelled out into the world.

Chapter Eleven

Wisdom

The mysteries of life
slip through the web
into the great expanse
of the mind.

To catch a mystery
is to reach for a star
and find you held it all the time.

Driving home, I felt my mind overcrowded with many thoughts and questions. Being in two worlds is sometimes unsettling. Jesus was in the car with me, as He often is, and generally we conversed about things important to me or were simply quiet.

Finally, I turned to Him and spoke. "Why would I be led to Yogananda when I already have you? I feel that, if I pursue this path, you might think that I have set you aside, and that is not how I feel at all. You are more real to me than air. I love you with all my heart and soul."

My thoughts moved on as if I were being pushed. More words came without thinking . . . "It never entered my mind that I would need another teacher to teach me spiritual ways."

"Ah, Brave Heart, there is more for you to learn—never ending. You did not go to college to learn from just one teacher. You gathered knowledge through the experiences of many. Make room for other masters in your heart.

"I do not speak of those who stifle your potential. You will know the masters meant for you by their ability to help you recognize your uniqueness and lead you to realize God within and without.

"I could teach you all things. But we want you to also remember what you once knew and build upon that wisdom."

"We?

"I and other masters."

"I think of you as more than a master—a Christed avatar."

"I am also and always one of the masters."

"If I had already accomplished learning in other lifetimes from other masters, why would I need to experience it all over again?"

"Wisdom is the fruit of experience from many lives."

I suddenly felt it necessary to stop the car. I couldn't focus and drive at the same time. I found a place to pull over and turned off the engine. I turned to Jesus, and He was looking off into the sky as if not really there at all. Then He raised His right hand into the air as if pointing to infinity.

He said, *"Wisdom flows through the universe, as in a river's fast current. You can only remember bits and pieces of wisdom but not all of it. It runs off your fingers like water and leaves only a residue, as you attempt to scoop it up. If you use a vessel to catch it, you gain more. Still, the wisdom overflows because of its abundance and spills out from your inability to comprehend or retain it. But there is, always and forever, more wisdom to be had."*

He rested both of his hands on His heart and turned to me and said,

"But God-realization does not rest with wisdom. It is only in jumping into the river that you become the river. It is only in surrendering to love that you become wise."

Then He rested His hands in His lap. I waited.

"Think, Brave Heart, how wisdom retained from past lives serves you well in the present. Consider how your innate knowledge of breath work has been natural for you from childhood, and how you suddenly remembered your healing gift, and you have the ability to realize the

emptiness of some techniques which simply bring about physical sensations not akin to spiritual experience, and how you sing some chants as if you already know the music, and the moments of familiarity with Barnabas, Yogananda, Sri Yukteswar and other Holy Ones. Pay attention to these moments. All these rememberings and so much more were ingrained in you lifetimes ago.

"Still, you did not come into this lifetime remembering, even though all wisdom already resides in you and all creation."

"Do I need to remember and know everything spiritual to get to my final goal, to God?" I felt myself letting go, dissolving.

"Not at all. . . . Listen carefully. . . . Stay with me. Brave Heart, you are not listening. I'm losing you."

All grew silent. I went where bliss exists. Then, as if a loud clang reverberated through my being, I took a breath, as if breath was now important, and I was back to the present once again. I felt ungrounded until I looked into Jesus' eyes and found refreshment and remembered His words, *"More than the body is the soul."* And I no longer supposed this body as mine or not mine.

Jesus continued, *"Wisdom is dominated by love. Many waters cannot quench love. Love dominates all. God is Love. God as Love leads to self-realization.*

"It is because of love, not wisdom, that you choose to come back to help people in their turmoil.

"As you know, Brave Heart, the essence of a godly life lies in the everyday living of life. Living life with love will be enough. Realize that."

"Sweet Jesus, my heart expands when I think of your presence in my life. I cannot fully express my gratefulness. Lately, I have had feelings of fear that I might lose this friendship, for I feel a nudge toward learning about other masters, and even more so the presence of God is growing ever-stronger within . . . "

He interrupted me and said . . . *"I am never far from you. I will never abandon you. God and I and the masters are one."*

As I let out a deep sigh, warmth flowed through me. I could only smile. Then I traveled on.

Chapter Twelve

The Return

"How does one become a butterfly?" she asked
pensively. *"You must want to fly so much that you are
willing to give up being a caterpillar."*

—Paulus

It had been a few months since my first visit to Song of
the Morning. I returned, hoping to relive the memory of my
first visit.

I take myself back in time to tell you of this second visit,
as easily as taking a breath. I know that I am being blessed
to be able to recall the past in writing these books, for since
my awakening my memory has not always served me well.

Upon arrival at the gate, I turn off the radio and roll
down the car windows to welcome it all back in. A blast of
fresh air, touched by the promise of spring, reaches within

and envelopes me with welcoming sweetness. I stop the car, relishing the embrace, and listen to silent songs of the morning harmonizing with bird songs, welcoming the beginnings of spring and me. I put my head out the window to look up into the trees to find the birds, and I see a beautiful network of branches replacing the snow-laden canopy of winter. They are barren now, with only a hint of green, budding lace, providing places for the singing birds to nest within their confines. Sunlight descends through white clouds and blue sky, filtering past the tree branches into the shadowy undergrowth. Only patches of snow remain, here and there, where shadows rest on the forest floor.

Wind flows through the car—as if Spirit is passing through, searching for things to do—in one window and out the other, in a steady flow, refreshingly cold on my face. Taking a deep breath, I start my car at a crawl. As I drive, I listen to the emerging forest waking up from its wintry slumber. I sing and am joined by the birds, who seem to echo a response. It's as if nature is in awe of itself, revelling in sacred syncopation.

Alone in nature, I feel no need to restrain my wonderment, as I might in the company of humans. Oh, if only I could feel this state of reverence all the time!

In reliving these memories, a poem I wrote about communing with nature in the timeless, present moment comes to mind.

ALL IN THE MOMENT

Ah blessed, sacred moment,
reveal yourself before you are spent;
broaden the view,
heighten the day,
gather the stars
to glitter the way;

smile the flowers,
bouquet the trees,
shine the raindrop,
warm the breeze;

fragrance the soil,
grow the grass . . .
all in the moment
before you pass.

Suddenly, I am at a standstill, as the road is a sea of mud. I realize that, until warmer weather arrives, melted snow cannot penetrate the frozen ground. Faced with challenging mire, I can only back up to get a good, long running start.

In my spotless, white car, I slip and slide through the mud, paying no mind now to all the beauty in the periphery. I have no choice but to plow through, without a thought for anything but a successful, safe arrival.

Then, coming to a place where ample sunlight reaches the road, I find it dry and mud-free. I stop my now-muddied chariot, relieved for making it thus far. Opening the car door, I step out for a stretch and look around. The awakening, yellow-green spring is a dramatic change from the white, snow-laden branches of last winter.

The birds are quieter now, as if contemplating my mad rush through the mud and scrutinizing my worthiness to hear their songs. I close my eyes and am moved to sing. The more I sing, the less I need breath. Losing myself in the singing, I become the song. Soon the birds join in. Suddenly, the wind stops blowing, beautiful, disharmonious sounds that can't be heard with physical hearing join us, and I am filled with the presence of Jesus.

Looking up, I behold glittering light, like angel dust, falling from out of the partly-cloudy, azure-blue sky, landing on Jesus, me and my muddied, white car. I laugh aloud as tears of joy flow from my eyes.

I have not come for any specific program this time, just a retreat for myself. So there is no hurry. I can linger here, within the joy, all day if I wish. That is, if no other cars come along to make me move.

I put off facing the next stretch of mud for only so long, then am urged to continue. After backing up as far as I dare, I speed up and plow through the next quagmire, bouncing from one rut to another, in order to keep from getting bogged down. I make my way from solid ground to solid ground, not stopping but plowing on. Finally, I reach my goal.

The lake, free of its wintry, icy coat, is grayed by its reflection of a progressively darkening sky and stirred up by a building wind. Canadian Geese glide down to land in the cold water. I shiver from the thought of it, but am very happy to arrive, and my spirit is not dampened by the increasing overcast and the threat of a spring storm.

As on my first visit to Song of the Morning, I stop at the dam and get out of my chariot to look over the simple railing to see the rushing waterfall. The strong winds and my impaired vestibular system cause me to lose my balance.

My mind is screaming, "I dare not fall." The wind is pushing me forward, so with all my will, I push against the railing, with my back against the wind, to regain inner and outer balance. I find myself leaning backward against my mud-blemished car, out of breath. Resting there, I slowly gain a sense of equilibrium, feeling increasingly secure.

Then, overcome by grief that my physical self is still not strong and normal, I let myself give in to tears. I stand there, tired from the long journey, remorseful now.

> *Oh . . . temple of mine,*
> *What of the blemishes I carry . . .*
> *The weathered intricacies of the body?*
> *Might I ignore them and they will vanish?*
> *What of the weakness of my temple?*
> *Why the pain?*
> *It is taking so long. . . .*

Gathering my dismay and holding it within, I leave the dam and head for the lodge . . . to the same bed I had before in the women's dorm. Thankfully, I have it all to myself once again.

I had hoped this visit would put me into another state of euphoria, like the last time I came here. Back then, I was elated at my accomplishments in the short time since my awakening. Now, soon after arriving, I am depressed because I don't feel I am physically bouncing back enough. I see only the dark of myself, and I trudge around as if everything is in my way.

The sky finally gives in to rain, and I lie down to rest, listening to the rolling thunder as it echoes my sorrow.

Then Jesus reminds me, *"The more you dwell on your distressing thoughts, the greater is your suffering."*

Glowing with brilliant, white, pulsating light, Jesus enfolds me in His expansive cocoon of white. I hear myself whisper, "Help me," then I simply fall asleep.

GRIEVING SONG

The storm of the night surrounds me,
Filling the darkened sky,
Flooding the earth with pouring rain,
In concert with my grieving cry.

Thunder rolls in the heavens.
Lightning pierces through the night.
Restless winds swirl fearsome,
In awesome flight.

The storm of my heart upon me
Opens its darkened vein
And joins the storm of wrath;
Tears flow like precious rain.

While the heaven's thunderous symphony
Clears the way for tomorrow's light,
It rains its cleansing bath
From out of this frightening night.

Then, hushed by the softening rainfall
As the storm overhead is calmed,
My heart feels the protection of angels,
And I finish my grieving song.

Refreshed by the storm in the heavens,
Renewed by the storm in my heart,
I will rise from my dreams in the morning
With a healed, fresh, tranquil start.

I sleep through the evening meditation and chanting. I sleep until very early morning, and now am awake, feeling cleansed and full of life, free of sorrow and ready to start over. I know Jesus has answered my prayer for help.

I put on my raincoat and go outside. Everything is greener, and brighter, as if it were laundered. The splendid storm has aroused the forest. I smell the fragrant pine trees . . . the clean air . . . the earth. I breathe it all in deeply, cleansing myself with its freshness. The sun is barely up and is lighting up the fringes of the fleeing, gray clouds with a touch of gold, as if to dismiss them with a kiss.

A song of thanksgiving rises up from me. It can't be stopped. It flows without words . . . just sacred sounds of praise . . . and I feel joy. There are no words to describe such things as this. Language and intellect are inadequate.

It is the way it is. And out of the joy comes laughter, bubbling up like a brook going the wrong way just for the fun of it.

I pocket an apple and decide to walk to the Christ Shrine. I don't know how far the shrine is or what I will find there, nor do I even care. I have no time restraints.

The forest is very inviting. Yet, I don't feel as though I am entering the forest, but that the forest is entering me. The path is of emerald-green moss, and is easy to follow. The wind is at my back and seems to be pushing me along. I walk for some time and find my strength waning, so I lay my raincoat upon the wet, mossy path and sit down. I tenderly feel the velvety surface, the cool dampness of the moss, and as I caress it, I am so drawn into its inviting comfort that I curl up, within the protection of my raincoat, and rest on it a while, holding converse with nature.

Oh, sweetness of the softness,
I feel gentleness in your endearing essence.
Your welcoming carpet of freshness,
Your emerald giving of heart, give me repose.

After a momentary, refreshing rest, I continue further into the forest. Truly there is a reason for this walk, for despite my weakened state, I do not give up and go back to the warmth of the lodge. I am drawn deeper into the forest. As I slowly walk, I can feel the energy and life of the forest. No dogma here, in this sanctuary of nature's great perfection.

I come to a bench, which reminds me to rest. But, with my raincoat to keep me dry, I sit, once again, upon the wet, mossy velvet. In my resting, I look around into the forest and imagine things not there, or are they? I look back on the long path from where I came and see no one. I look into the forest and see nothing unusual. Still, I feel someone other than Jesus, with me. Not unsettled, I eat my apple. Then rested, I move on and soon come to the Christ Shrine.

I love simplicity. There is no gold gracing the shrine, at the end of the trail. Simply and profoundly, the beauty of nature, the blue sky, great white pines, emerging leaf buds and fiddle-head ferns, bird songs, the smell of the freshness of the morning . . . and Spirit . . . are there.

There is a post supporting a lovely picture of Jesus. This is the Christ Shrine. I am overwhelmed by the simplicity of it all. Encircling the shrine within my arms . . . I gather Jesus close to my heart . . . and His love flows through my body . . . and I sing over and over . . .

Ah . . . Holy Jesus,
Friend, forever faithful,
You make of my pathway
Safe and ever-narrow.

Ah . . . Holy Jesus,
All of nature gathers,
Praising God together.

And I sing on and on—raising my voice as my pain transforms into melody. Other voices join in, a bit off-key, above and below my singing, as if all of nature is singing. And Jesus is there.

Over and over, we sing the words, slower . . . faster . . . louder . . . softer . . . over and over, and our chanting goes on and on . . . flowing as a running stream, or incense smoke, or clouds up in the sky . . . merging with nature . . . with spirit . . . as one.

As I slowly walk out of the forest, refreshed and strengthened, I hear "home at last," as surely as daylight fills the sky.

Chapter Thirteen

Let Your Religion Be Love

What divine drink wouldst thou have, my God, from this overflowing cup of my life?

Is it Thy delight to see Thy creation through my eyes and to stand at the portals of my ears silently to listen to Thine own eternal harmony?

Thy world is weaving words in my mind and Thy joy is adding music to them. Thou givest Thyself to me in love and then feelest Thine own entire sweetness in me.

—Gitanjali, verse 65, by Tagore

Eventually, I went back to work part-time, and initially, it so drained me physically that, when I went home in the evenings, I often did only what had to be done and then rested in meditation. Still, this did not weaken my determination to heal, for I would push myself into more and more physical activity, and very slowly I gained strength until, finally, I was able to work full-time.

At home, while I was caught up in things needing doing and people to see for healing and counseling, as well as at work, I was able to meditate in what I called a "waking" meditation. At those times, I felt as if I were two people, one performing activities, and the other fully aware of God in peace beyond thought, or in quiet communication with Jesus. I still do this today.

When I could, I visited Song of the Morning for personal quiet retreats on weekends, once I realized you didn't have to sign up for a class.

Jesus had good reasons to encourage my visits to Song of the Morning, for I needed a place where I would be free to grow spiritually without restraint and learn from, compare and see the significance of other masters and spiritual paths.

I was breaking away from identifying myself exclusively with my religious upbringing, which had proven beneficial as a foundation for my spiritual development but now seemed to stand in the way of it and my healing work. It was as if I had taken one step and now was taking additional steps, each rung higher and higher, as in Jacob's ladder leading to heaven.

When I started going to Song of the Morning Retreat in 1998, I didn't always feel that I fit in. Something was not quite right, yet I felt compelled to be there. I missed the structure of the liturgical services to which I had become accustomed, and Sweet Jesus' words were rarely read. Sunday services were based more on the spiritual director's reminiscences of his own spiritual path than on Yogananda's teachings.

It was never a specific person or what was spoken at the services that kept me coming back. I truly did not think I could fit the mold there, or anyone's mold. I felt done with dogma. Sometimes I thought I needed to fit in, and other times I felt like I was floating on a sea of bliss, content within my Self.

After reliving those moments, Jesus, ever-present, instilled in my heart, *"Patience, Dear One. The structure at Song of the Morning is hidden for now and, when it is found, it will be like welcoming home a lost child.*

"When you think you haven't found the perfect fit, it's because you are looking outside of yourself and not within. Where you fit is not a place.

"Seek ye first the kingdom of God within. You do not find God while concentrating on stagnant dogma.

"Ah, Brave Heart, even so, everyone can learn and grow from reasonable communal worship. Learning never ends and comes from every experience you have ever had."

With Jesus' words, I envisioned Song of the Morning on a future sunshiny day as a bustling center of light and love . . . a place to find oneself in the very core of one's soul . . . a place to worship, as an individual or a community. A pleasant, warm feeling came over me.

"Sweet Jesus, many confide in me that they are confused by all the religions, teachers and techniques out there and don't know where they fit and which way to go. Most of the time, in my healing work and mentoring, I simply listen to them and they seem to find their own answers. Other times, I address their concerns with words that flow out of my mouth."

"You see, answers are within! Listen to your inner wisdom."

"Why do we vacillate so much when we know the answers?"

"Simply human nature; a way of learning through relearning."

"I've been thinking . . . that it seems . . . when we imitate the practices of others, some of us remain caught up in repetition, routine, techniques and rituals long after we are made aware that we should move on.

"It is very difficult to change one's beliefs or practices, even if new ones are called for. And it's hard to give up old friends, even though new ones may be just around the corner. It's as if there is an attachment to the worthiness of the past. Since I left my church, I experience a sadness when I think on it, which lingers to this day, like grieving for a lost family.

"In the quest for God, the spiritual path, or journey, we choose has to be uniquely our own and guided, at least in part, from within. Yet, most people continue on as they have in the past, fearful of change and fearful of relying on intuition for natural, spiritual progressions that befit them as individuals.

"Like a baby bird sitting on the edge of its nest afraid to

take that first flight, many are afraid of where they might land."

Jesus lets me continue on as if He is pretending to be learning something new, while fully attentive, smiling. Or maybe He is putting the words in my heart.

"At another time, Jesus, you shared with me what Gandhi said, 'In reality, there are as many religions as individuals.' Gandhi knew we all have different paths, and he also knew that we all have a common goal: God-realization, enlightenment.

"Because each person has a unique relationship with God and a sacred right to make their own choices, there should be no comparisions here—no judging of another's path—between individuals or between nations.

"Yet people, left to their own devices, don't always know what will help them find God, and even when they do know, they may benefit from being with others who have similar spiritual needs. So on one's spiritual path, one may find guidance and support by associating with a religious institution or guru. Some of them encourage spiritual growth at a pace that is beneficial for the individual who actively seeks God. A person only needs to search to find the best fit. What is right for one may not be right for another."

Often I go from speaking of Jesus to speaking of God or the Holy Spirit, as if all three were one, for I believe Jesus and the Holy Spirit each reflect divine attributes of the one, all-inclusive, living God. Each are omnipresent, omniscient and omnipotent.

Some people relate to Jesus more easily than God, for Jesus was man. And the Holy Spirit lays claim on us, comforts us, and fills us with Truth and Christ Consciousness. God encompasses everything: from the infinitesimal particles of creation and the space between; to the little, creepy, crawly things, and all of us; right on up to all the stars in the sky, seen and unseen, and infinite love.

"The Retreat fills my need to be alone—introverted. I can be separate from its splintered structure. Even the spiritual director doesn't seem to be aware of me. It's as if I can be as invisible as I want to be."

Jesus breaks in upon my discourse and says, *"Keeping to your self is not introversion! Introversion is hiding your light under a bushel basket . . . it is not a spiritual state.*

"You are experiencing spirituality on many levels, not just inward. You are not shrinking from the world. You are realizing and assimilating new truths on many levels."

I have to stop for a moment. Jesus' words fill me with such sweet bliss.

In sharing these experiences of my life, there comes to me an awareness of the beauty and worthwhileness of the whole journey.

And now, I settle myself to take up where I left off in expressing my thoughts—for I feel He wants that—and again words just come.

"Religion has played its part in controlling the way people relate to God and each other, sometimes through fanatic, rigidly-held beliefs."

At this point, Jesus interrupts me again, *"Fanaticism obstructs growth. Having the same God is what binds all religions together. There is only one God. Diversity does not serve God. Diversity is dualism.*

"More and more, there are many who realize that the world's religions are, through their opposition with each other, defeating the roles of their masters and of God to save and nourish mankind. These individuals are falling away from organized religions and are on their own."

Feeling Jesus has something more to say, I wait in anticipation. And when it comes, His ethereal form flows within an aura of silent, colorful flame, and His fragrance intensifies.

"The foundation of the religious self is the realization that your inner and outer self are one with God and creation. Grace is added unto you through your love."

"In the Bible, I read that pure religion is to visit the afflicted and to keep oneself unstained from the world.[41] There is hardly any other usage of the word "religion" in the Bible. It would seem that pure religion is love in action."

"Open the door of your heart sanctuary; religion comes from the heart. Let your religion be Love. God is Love."

My heart overflowed as He spoke of love. All sense of being in a physical body was lifted as if it were a mere layer of veil. Time passed.

Suddenly, I found myself envisioning an unstained "Garden of Eden". For some reason, I knew it for what it was and saw, with vibrant clarity, the flora and fauna and colors of the garden—lit up with a profuse radiance—the river flowing through, the animals, the sky, the brilliant flowers. And as I write, this very moment, I am smelling their sweet fragrances. They fill me. I can only carry it within. And there is such freedom and peace.

Next, a glimpse of "Heaven" came before me, another unstained garden . . . of paradise promised. It was flowing with all colors and no colors, all movement and no movement. There was no physicality, nor fixed shapes or forms. The peace was beyond imagining, and it is only through the mind of my soul that I can do any justice in the telling of this, for my physical body was not present there.

Suddenly, time seemed to back up to leave a space between the "Garden of Eden" and "Heaven", and present earth was shown to me from afar. I saw shades of light and dark. I was made aware that, in our disregard for Mother Earth, we are setting aside the spirituality of nature and its sacred role in our lives.

The vision continued on to show me the devastating result of further neglect. Then in the silence of my soul, I was made to realize that, in the light that radiates from all good actions, there is hope. Thoughts flashed through my mind and left a burning reminder within me of the crucial importance of our relationship with nature, and I was made aware that through love we increase the light on our planet.

Becoming aware of Jesus' presence, the visions ended as these thoughts entered my heart, *"One who walks in the awareness of God sheds light on the world, for they are in communion with the sacredness of the world and all it contains."*

"Ah, Sweet Jesus . . . how can I express that nature is a sacred extension of our all-inclusive Creator? How can I help people experience . . . realize . . . that, if we touch a leaf, we have touched God? It seems we need constant reminders.

"I know that, through loving attunement with nature, we become aware of the ways in which our modern way of life, the heavy footprint of man, is distorting the web of life on earth. Yet, if we make a determined effort to protect and refresh Mother Earth and cast love's light upon all she holds within her keep, we in turn are gifted with abundance and beauty.

"In the Findhorn Community in Scotland[42], the productivity of their gardens is increased by lovingly communicating and working in harmony with Mother Nature and her nature spirits. We all need to do this.

"Unconditional, universal love that includes all beings and all of nature in its embrace is the path we must pursue if we are to realize our cherished goals: health, happiness, and peace on earth."

Then it was over, the loving presence of Jesus vanished and, for a short time, I was left breathless, as if He had taken my breath with Him and then had released it back to me.

Chapter Fourteen

Yogananda

*Ah, holy man, my sight is filled
from your single star,
yet I cannot hear your voice
in the shining silence,
however strong your pull
within my heart.*

*As I walk in the midst
of infinite moments,
may I sing upon the gentle breeze,
to shower you with words of love.*

On a summer afternoon, upon arriving at the Retreat for a visit, I go to the lodge, where I always have the same room, the same bed. Sweet evening meditation and a sound sleep pass quickly. Morning arrives and breakfast has been served. I am simply relaxing.

I find a quiet place outdoors, sitting at a picnic table that overlooks the sparkly lake, and I am about to start reading a book I found in the lodge library about quieting the mind.

Relaxing in the warmth of the sun, I am aware of someone watering the flowers. Upon finishing, he walks over to me and introduces himself as George Johnston, whom I later find out tends the organic vegetable garden and lives near the Retreat. He sits down and we talk for a while.

He asks what I am reading, then explains how to quiet the mind through meditation. He asks if I have read *Autobiography of a Yogi* by Yogananda.[43] We discuss the book, and I realize what a wealth of spiritual knowledge George has to share.

I had bought the book on one of my recent visits, and I read it through swiftly, as one would read fiction. Yogananda's experiences and those of his master, Sri Yukteswar, enthralled me. Then someone said that they thought it was very deep and hard to understand. Thinking I might have missed something, since I still was having difficulty remembering things, I reread it several more times, and its truths were gently instilled.

From then on, whenever I returned to the Retreat, George and I found time to walk together, along the sparkling, sunlit lake or under tree canopies of vibrant, autumn-colored leaves or on the emerald, mossy path leading to the Christ shrine, mostly in silence, each with our own thoughts, unaware of the preciousness of our relationship.

CAGE OF TREES

Along the enchanted, mossy path,
There stands a cage of trees,
Wherein we stood, the two of us,
Among the golden leaves.

It took from us our growing old,
In a peaceful, gentle way,
Gathering all of nature round,
As in enchanted play.

An orchestrated, etheric flow
Blew wind and falling leaves,
While birds, embraced in sunlit glow,
Played within the cage of trees.

Spirit and Nature were with us then,
Where everything was light,
As we discovered how day ends
And how begins the night.

Our friendship seemed quite natural . . . not rushed, not demanding. I liked that he respected my silence. Placed in my life, he carried spiritual energy that enhanced my being.

At Song of the Morning, Christmas is celebrated with a six-hour meditation during the week, a service and a dinner. Even though I chose to be with my family over Christmas, I did make plans to go to the Retreat for the New Year's celebration and stay into the next week for Yogananda's birthday.

I was asked if I would like to sing a karaoke Christmas carol for their New Year's Eve musical concert. I chose "Lo, How a Rose E'er Blooming." I had not sung in front of people since my awakening. For me, accepting this challenge felt like a big step forward.

On New Year's Eve, I sat on a chair, in my red plaid Christmas dress, to sing. My voice was clear, and my breath control was as easy as a leaf carried by the wind a great distance. It was a surprise for everyone that I could sing.

When I finished singing, I sat down on a floor cushion in the back of the room. Amy, a ninety-year-old, tiny lady sitting next to me, asked me in a high, soft voice if I would like to come to her house to hear her play the piano. I couldn't imagine that she could play well; she looked frail. But I accepted.

The next afternoon, a few other invitees and I arrived at her home. George was renting a room from her so he joined us. As we sat down, she spread her music across the piano, settled herself to be able to reach the pedals, and with total command, this tiny ninety-year-old attacked the piano, playing Beethoven and Bach! On and on, she played with great skill and feeling. Then, I closed my eyes, let myself enter the music and flowed with it.

* * *

The evening of Yogananda's birthday, as I went into the Retreat dining room, I felt myself shift into a state of meditative euphoria in which I was aware of being one with everything. My memory clear . . . I remember it vividly, as if I were back there again.

Almost startled, I looked up as I entered. Everything and everyone in the dining room was lit up, as if a light had been turned on, outlining every form in brilliance beyond what was physically possible. All movement slowed down. As I sat with others for dinner, everything was clean and bright and stood out. I felt surrounded and permeated by the light, unsure where I ended and it began.

People were chatting and eating, seemingly in a manner that was not different from the norm, and yet I saw it differently. As I watched the slowed performance, no one seemed aware of this phenomenon, nor was I moved to share it.

George, unaware of what I was experiencing, sat at my right, and we ate a beautiful meal within the glow, in slow motion. . . . As everyone was eating, I saw that each mouthful was truly an act of devotion, yet they were totally unaware of this.

Through the open kitchen door, I watched Carrie, who loved making desserts, place dessert on individual dishes with loving care. I was mesmerized by her undeviating focus on her task. She was simply, meticulously placing pieces of pie on individual plates, with unswerving devotion to her task. I could feel her reverence. She glowed within the scene, unaware of everything around her, unaware of me watching. Her movements were in slow motion, as each crumb was removed or put in its place, each piece of pie perfectly centered on the plate. The light of God poured forth grace through her into plate after plate of pie, as she orchestrated perfection, and energy resonated outward, everywhere, encompassing all. This was truly soul food in its highest form.

Within the moments between moments, I realized, from her beautiful, loving essence, that she was preparing to serve God. And I realized that truly every action we take is in the oneness and presence of God. Observing the action encompassed in the brightness as time slowed down, I was amazed at the unity of the whole as life went on.

I watched as each person was silently attended to. I watched this beautiful, egoless woman devotionally serve this dessert to each guest, as if it were being placed before God. I watched as they ate it, seemingly unaware of its blessed state. I remember being served this love-filled pie. I don't remember what kind of pie it was. I don't remember eating it.

This phenomenon of brilliance-seeing and the euphoric feelings that accompany it has occurred in many instances throughout my life. And sometimes, as if waiting to be noticed, this light surprises me in unexpected places, in everyday life. We dwell in it, most often unaware.

The meal ended and everyone stayed around the table to chat. No one had even mentioned that it was Yogananda's birthday. I thought it was odd that this was a yoga retreat center, reportedly based on Yogananda's teachings, and they didn't mention or publicly announce a celebration for his birthday.

I couldn't help but ask, "Why do you celebrate Jesus' birth with a six-hour meditation, and the New Year with a three-hour meditation, and for Yogananda's birthday, nothing?"

I received a sound retort for that one with the reply, "What do you want, presents?" I said no more, but for some reason it bothered me.

I admired how Yogananda referred to Jesus as an avatar of supreme magnitude in his book, *Autobiography of a Yogi*. It felt comfortable that a new teacher was becoming near and dear to me, even with Jesus at my side.

I was pleased when, finally, I was told the evening meditation was to be devoted to Yogananda. Before it started, we were each handed a flower.

I immediately held the flower up to my nose to smell it. George came over to me and said, "For this celebration we keep the fragrance for the Master, so we don't smell it." I love to smell flowers—they seem to speak to me—but I reluctantly abstained from smelling it any further. However, I looked upon and felt its loveliness. And then, hesitating, I wondered if I should have left even those perceptions to the Master also. How could I restrain myself from such beauty in hand? I held the flower and attempted to not pay attention to it.

During the service, at the appropriate time, I laid the flower on the altar as an offering to Yogananda in celebration of his birthday. I knelt there for a moment in prayer and thanked Yogananda for his presence in my life.

When I returned to my place, I suddenly felt very cold and looked to see if the entrance door was open. It wasn't open. My tinnitus became deafening, like a train rushing through, and immediately I had a headache. Time stood still. I turned my head toward the altar, and I saw Yogananda before me in shining, ethereal form—with welcoming arms, smiling at me—accompanied by a heavenly fragrance of flowers so aromatic it overpowered the flowers already in the room. It entered me, I felt it throughout my body and I could taste the fragrance in my saliva.

The noise, the pain and the cold simply were no more. As I kept my eyes fixed on Yogananda, I felt overwhelming love, and silent tears of joy flowed down my face as the fragrance lingered within me. And as I breathed the fragrance over and over, I felt a vacuum building within me. My pelvic floor clamped shut, and energy shot up my spine, radiating throughout my body.

Into the source of all God made,
in boundless void displayed!
What was hidden from my mortal eyes
I saw through the eye of my soul.

Ah, sweet communion this did impart
on the strings of my immortal heart.
As if I were an instrument to be played,
what filled my heart was clearly conveyed.

All this as Yogananda stood there with arms outstretched, smiling, seemingly thanking and welcoming me. "Home at last" resonated in my heart. And all the while, I was oblivious to the birthday-commemoration meditation continuing on around me.

Keeping this experience to myself, for I did not know how much I should share with my new friends or even what to say, I simply grew closer to Yogananda and Song of the Morning.

Chapter Fifteen

Divine Orchestration

I can love you with all my heart and soul,
my very being,
and still have the same intensity
of love to love others,
left over from when I loved you,
ever constant, instantly renewed . . .
for God is love and is never diminishing.

After the holidays, I wrote a thank-you note to George for his Christmas card. He wrote back to me and I wrote back to him, and on and on. When I would put a letter in the mailbox I knew in my heart that I would receive a reply very soon. Since I did not visit the Retreat as often in the wintry weather, the letter writing was very welcome. I didn't think of it in this way, but our writing was keeping us connected.

In May of 1998, I began to simplify my life. I sensed a need to rid myself of unnecessary possessions, simplify my surroundings, and complete unfinished projects. I felt suspended between wanting stability and following my soul's longing to move on.

I rented out my lovely home, stored some furniture and gave the rest to my bewildered children. Then I bought a small trailer with a private dock upstream on the Manistee River. I thought it might serve as a haven to come to if I were to start traveling as an occupational therapist again.

The move was good therapy, a cleansing within and without. I went from my large home to a trailer I respectfully called "my rinky dink."

Throughout the trailer, I washed the paneling, primed it, and papered it with embossed paper, which then needed to be painted. Nearly every wall in the place was worked on four times.

There was an abundance of insects in the trailer. So one day, I stopped what I was doing and went outside. I walked around the trailer slowly, several times, talking in reverence to their guiding intelligence, asking them to keep all of their kind from entering my trailer and telling them that I would honor their natural places outside. From then on, there were no more insects in the trailer.

I loved the new setting on the river. I could swim there. The river was too swift at my prior home, but here it was inviting me to enter it.

THE RIVER

Slipping off the dock
into the cold, flowing journey,
I find the bottom quickly.
Neck high in the freezing current,
the river consumes me.

The current, strong, pushes me.
I stand fast against its strength,
keeping courage.
Then. . . I flow with it,
knowing I can turn into it
when'ere I choose.

I am not put off by its power
and know it for its healing nature.
Then, I turn against it,
swimming against the trial.
My strength is up to it,
and I smile in the conquering.

Going with the flow
is not always the answer.
Standing against the current
can also be an answer.

And with willing it to happen and my efforts to make it
so, I was getting ever stronger, day by day.

The rehabilitation company that employed me closed,
and I was laid off, eligible for unemployment. I found I had

a lot of leisure time on my hands, which I enjoyed immensely.

I did a month-long work-exchange for room and board, at Song of the Morning. I thought, by doing that, I could determine if I might want to make a permanent move to the Retreat.

But a few months later, I decided I wasn't ready for retirement, and one night, I adamantly affirmed: "I am going to find a job that is perfect for me in every way."

The next day, I called a company that employs traveling therapists and asked if they had any occupational therapy jobs available. They had job openings in Arizona, Illinois, South Carolina and Kentucky, but when I asked if they had anything in Michigan, apologetically they said they had one, but it was "way up in Gaylord." I joyously replied, "Perfect!" Gaylord is a short drive from Song of the Morning. Further, they reluctantly said it was "only part-time." "Perfect!" I shouted. Part-time work was just what I wanted. Thank you, God.

On returning to my rinky-dink trailer on the river after a successful job interview, I had a message on my answering machine from a friend of my daughter, who had recently visited me there. She wanted to buy my trailer and, by 4:00 p.m. that afternoon, I had the money in the bank.

I bought a lease on a lot in the new Clear Light Community development at Song of the Morning with part of the money. Then I called my aged friend Amy, the pianist, told her I had a job in the area and asked her if she had a vacant room to let. She did, so I prepared to move in with her, her cat, and George. Now I was down to living in one room.

The sequence of events had to have been divinely orchestrated. I had been assigned to an occupational therapy position in my hometown, moved from a good-sized home to a small trailer to rid myself of possessions I didn't need, soon got a new assignment near the Retreat, and that very day sold my trailer! A place to live was provided, close to the retreat, with new friends. God was truly taking good care of me. And thus, a way was opened for me to be where I was supposed to be.

Chapter Sixteen

Magical Moments

Within the lacy, wintry wood,
an enchanting place to be,
there stands a cottage,
low and fair, amongst the giant trees.

Within, the owner—aged, kind—
lets out rooms to devotees,
provides a haven lovingly
in sweet Amens of peace.

Late September of 1999, on a sunshiny autumn day, I moved into Amy's home, just two miles from Song of the Morning. I had downsized from a spacious home to a trailer to a single room, sharing a bathroom with a man, all within a short time. I soon felt awkward and wondered if I had made the right move.

I had to learn the rules set down by Amy. She was a yogi, so I was told, but I wasn't sure what that meant. She was very contemplative in her way of living, meditating much of the time and often tending her garden, reading, or playing the piano. I learned much from her.

On the first day, knowing I was responsible for my own meals and with my own space in the refrigerator, I went into the kitchen to make myself something to eat. George came out of his room and, to my surprise, said to me, "So, what are we having for dinner?" I wasn't sure what to say, but he quickly added, "You cook and I will clean up." Sounded good to me.

I learned to be as quiet as a mouse in the kitchen and everywhere else in the house. Silence was the rule. There was no television. Our rooms and a bathroom were what we rented, and that was where we were supposed to be, except for preparing our meals and eating at the dinner table.

It was not fully clear to me why I was so compelled to be near Song of the Morning. You might think I wanted to be closer to George; however, my desire to be at the Retreat started when I first came to Song of the Morning, six months prior to meeting him. I was, for the most part, content being alone and had kept to myself most of the time, so it took me that long to notice George, though he was there daily.

Nor was it the spiritual direction provided at the Retreat at the time that was drawing me. Something else was calling me—maybe a desire to seek refuge from the world, perhaps the energy of the place or Yogananda.

I had just uprooted myself once more, and now I was

already having mixed feelings about where I belonged and my future. Sometimes I felt like I was right where I was supposed to be, and other times I wondered why I had moved away from family once again. It was as if I was not attached to anything at all. Most often that felt good, and other times the uncertainties would only be alleviated by my talks with Jesus, my breath work, and meditation.

After a time, all of my uncertainties began to weigh heavily on me, and I felt tension building within me. I had to get rid of it. One day, instead of turning to Jesus, I sat down to journal, and in lamentation, words poured onto the paper . . . as if they were not entirely my words. Feelings and concerns about the choices I had made recently filled several pages, and the pages moaned with heaviness.

Unable to sort out and find meaning in the written words, I rose from the task heavy laden, tore the pages from the journal, folded and put them in my pocket, and left the house. I went to the Retreat and started to walk swiftly down a forest trail as if I had a destination. With tears flowing, I cried aloud to God and Jesus, continuing to vent my uncertainties . . . trying to find meaning as to why I had uprooted myself to come to Song of the Morning.

I cannot bring myself to give you the words I wrote and voiced. They spoke only of my unsettled self, lamenting in my own sorrow and tears . . . releasing, releasing.

And then another new friend, Victor, who worked at the Retreat, was suddenly walking beside me, in step with my hurried pace, quietly accompanying me on my quest for understanding, quietly listening to my ranting on and on.

I became breathless for want of air. Victor's peacefulness became as if Jesus were present in him. Suddenly realizing this, I took a deep gasp of air, sighed it out and was calmed. Smiling at Victor, I simply stopped, stood there looking quietly at him and the surrounding forest, then watched him go on his way until he was out of sight.

Once Victor left, I sat down on the trail, took my list out of my pocket, and as I read my lamentations, I began to slowly tear each one into tiny pieces and throw them into the air. I watched them float, as if the weight of them was no more. And after the process of letting them go, a cadence of adamant resolve began to take the place of lamentation. In its grasp were declarations of sound intentions. I felt increased lightness and strength flowing through me as I vowed:

I declare that I am steadfast upon my path to God.
I declare that I have the courage to be my true self.
I declare that I am a loving conduit for God's healing grace.
I declare that I will be of service to humanity and the world we live in.
I declare self-realization for myself!

And now, Jesus, in all the shining glory that I can tolerate, says, *"Ah, Brave Heart, live these declarations! Even though they are personal, there are many who will be able to relate to your lamenting and will be guided to create their own affirmations.*

"Look within yourself. All you need is within. You are where you are supposed to be."

So many times Jesus had told me that I was where I was supposed to be and it only mattered what I did with my circumstances. Yet I didn't always remember this concept when I needed it. Could it be that wherever we are is where we need to be and that our circumstances have been attracted to us by our thoughts and serve a purpose in furthering the growth of our soul and the souls of others?

One weekend, there was a program at the Retreat to which I felt drawn. Coming from a conservative Christian background, from which I was escaping, this weekend proved to be one of startling, new revelations for me.

At one point, while we were all outside standing in a circle, the presenter led us in a creative visualization. We were to call upon and envision a merkaba. No description of what a merkaba looks like was given. A vision came to me, but I was abruptly drawn from it by another participant excitedly exclaiming that she had a bloody nose. I walked over to her, touched the side of her nose, the flow stopped, and I stepped back into the circle.

Then I saw what could best be described as two pyramid forms of light, one upside down within the other, forming a star. The pyramid-star rotated so fast that it flattened out into something like a glorious, sunset scene upon a great lake, only to be transformed into the pyramid-star form again. Still nothing was said about what a merkaba is or looks like.

We went from there into a building called the "wheelhouse." Sitting in a circle on chairs, I saw the floor in the center of the room opening up, and out came a person in ethereal form. He said to me, "My name is Sebastian, and I have been waiting for you." Strangely, those words felt familiar to me, as if I had heard them many times in the past. I almost laughed aloud.

He had sandaled feet and wore a tunic, a mantle and a sword. Behind him, coming up from beneath the floor, were what best can be described as "little people," all dressed alike in colors of earth. I cannot begin to tell you how this affected me.

I was excitedly trying to explain to the other participants all that was happening, while the surprised looks on some of their faces demonstrated fear. The "little people" were walking around the room and placing themselves behind seated people. It was delightful.

I had never seen such nature spirits before, although I have acknowledged the wind and weather at times and spoken to insects', plants' and animals' higher natures and, of course, my pink angel and several spirit friends.

Another layer of veil was being lifted; I felt lighter, freer somehow.

Since then, I have learned from Sebastian that he had come to help me as an infant by entering the family dog. I have no memory of those times, but a few years ago, an older sister shared with me what she remembered of those early years when the family dog cared for me until I was two. She was but five or six years old when I was born and naturally had no idea it was Sebastian.

Sebastian also told me it was he who came as the Labrador that visited me when I first began to live with my foster parents, and again as Rusty, who taught me to meditate. My foster mother remembers the Labrador's visits but does not know of Sebastian.

Sebastian told me he had been a spiritual guide to me in a past life when I was called Saint Ta by the local people because of my work as caregiver of abandoned children.

I have had a few visions of that past lifetime, but I never paid much attention to them, for I didn't understand visions or consider the possibility of past lives. I thought of them as sweet, recurring dreams.

However, one stands out. I was gathered with children outdoors, and we were having a meager meal, seated on the ground under a lone tree. The landscape was stark and barren. As we were sitting there, we could see Sebastian coming from afar. Some of the children rushed to greet him. He always brought us the means to barter for food, and stories to share. He was as if a soldier-saint, always with his sword in a sheath at his side. The children loved him as much as I.

I was worried becaused there was no food to share with him. I relied mostly on the local people to bring food when they could. Presently there was little to be had.

I shouldn't have been worried, for as soon as he joined

us, one small child went up to him and tore off a tiny portion of his bread and gave it to him. And before I knew it, each child did the same. He had his fill.

I recall that sanitation was a huge problem, and there were several babies. Also there were older children helping out, who I sensed had been with me as orphans and remained with me long after they could have left.

Although I remain curious about Sebastian, the "little people," and what more there might be, for now, I choose not to dwell on past lives, for thinking about them distracts me from what needs to be accomplished in the here and now. But I take great pleasure in visiting with Sebastian and the "little people."

I love walking in the forest at Song of the Morning. It gives me peace and makes me more aware of eternity, for time slows down. The forest is like a garden of God.

Yogananda composed many beautiful, devotional songs, to be chanted over and over for divine communion. One of my favorites, which I often sing while walking in the forest, has the words "Spirit and nature dancing together." What a delightful image this brings to mind . . . God, as Spirit, dancing with nature, infusing it with divine essence, causing living things to evolve toward glorious expressions of beauty and intelligence.

And further, imagine Spirit dancing with you—your heart manifesting love and infinite awareness, and your rational mind, which only perceives finite things, following the guidance of your heart.

In this holy dance, spurred on by ever-increasing realizations of the divinity within ourselves and all creation, we awaken in God. Ah . . . what joy!

About a month after my visit with Sebastian and the "little people," I thought it would be interesting to go to hear a woman speak who claimed to be channeling Joan of Arc. I had never witnessed such an event and was curious about the channeling aspect.

Much later, I asked George to explain channeling for this book, and he wrote the following:

"The terms 'channeling' and 'mediumship' have almost the same meaning. In the past, people who contacted spirits, especially those of departed family members, were called mediums. Then, starting in the nineteen seventies, many books were written that contained information from beings in the spirit world about life after death, metaphysics, and prophesied events, such as earth changes. Psychics who received this information began to be called channelers, and the process of receiving it was called channeling.

"Usually a channeler either consciously communicates with a spirit being but is unable to see it, or becomes a passive vessel, often unconscious, so that a spirit can use their vocal cords to speak or their hands to record messages.

"In either case, some channeled messages are true and come from great spiritual beings, some contain lies and are intended to deceive, and many are from spirits who have access to certain kinds of knowedge but are not infallible. Unlike the process of receiving information from beings who appear in visions or supernatural visitations, in channeling, the source of the information is invisible to the channeler and it is often impossible to determine if it is really who it says it is, if it has a high, low, or ordinary degree of spiritual development, and if it can be trusted to tell the truth.

"Only through clear spiritual insight and sound reasoning can one discern the nature of an invisible being or the value of what it says. Also, while some messages are straightforward and fit in with the spiritual teachings of enlightened masters, others are difficult to evaluate because truth and fiction are mixed together and the fiction is presented with such skill that it looks like truth.

"For these reasons, channeled messages should be carefully considered before being integrated into one's belief system, always keeping in mind that the most valuable and trustworthy information is that which is given in love and elevates one's consciousness."

I had not heard the term "channeling" until my later years and even then didn't really know what channeling was nor pay it much mind, but when I learned more about it, I realized my communion with Jesus is not channeling. For when I communicate with Jesus, I see Him in ethereal human form or as light, and I am not unconscious, but rather in superconscious oneness with Him—in an expanded state of consciousness that is loving and blissful. Jesus does not take over my body or personality. Nor did He, until I reached the age of sixty-two, ever give me messages for others. It was simply a personal, loving relationship.

When I arrived to hear the channeler, I decided to sit in the back of the room. Soon I was progressively beginning to feel miserable. The session was very unsettling for me. I felt as if I was being set upon by negative energies that were not for my highest good. I cannot say if it was from the channeler or someone or something else. I desperately needed to clear myself.

I left without delay before it was over, met George at the Retreat, where we had planned to eat dinner, and told him I needed to go home. There, in a meditative consciousness, I cleared major entities from myself.

While doing so . . . Yogananda burst out of the ethers in his orange robe, rushing toward me, shaking a fist with a finger extended straight at me, and in a booming voice said,

"NO MORE! NO MORE! GO WITH THE KNOWING AND LEARN FROM THE DOING!"

Suddenly my lungs filled with air charged with his energy. I couldn't breathe out, and I didn't want to. The moments seemed as if forever.

These were Yogananda's very first words to me! Then, with a smile that he seemingly could not hold back, he vanished.

Ever present, Jesus said, *"He told you good."*

* * *

While I was working in a nearby nursing home, I was asked to evaluate a patient who was paralyzed and on a ventilator. I was told he was Buddhist. Nursing staff assumed I was a Buddhist because I live at Song of the Morning. They weren't aware the Retreat is based on the teachings of Yogananda and that, although it welcomes members of all religions, it is not Buddhist. They thought I would relate better with the patient than another occupational therapist.

Upon observation, I found that he could move his right forearm, and flex and extend his hand, and had a moderate grip. Other than that, about all he could do was nod his head and turn it slightly. Because he was on a ventilator a good share of the time, which pumped air into a tracheal cannula (an opening in the throat), he could not speak and hadn't for over a year. He should have been in the vent unit but there was no room. He was middle-aged and had been an avid computer user.

When I first saw him, he was positioned on his right side and arm. I immediately instructed the nurses not to position him on his only useful side during the day.

I asked his girl friend to bring in his computer, and soon it was hooked up to the Internet. We positioned the computer on a cart, which could be brought up to within his range of vision. His keyboard was placed near his right side, where he could also work the mouse. His girl friend helped him email friends and family. She was grateful for being able to do something for him.

I made a night splint to support and protect his right hand and wrist, and taught his girl friend how to exercise his arms and hands and how to calm him with energy work and massage.

During treatment, I did all the talking, and he would nod in response. Because he was Buddhist, I guessed at what he might be interested in. I spoke to him about my relationship with Jesus. He seemed interested. I spoke to him of my beliefs and about Song of the Morning and my getting to know more about Yogananda and other religions. Daily, on and on, I spoke of my thoughts on philosophical subjects.

One day, it dawned on me that, if we were to plug the tracheal cannula while he was off the vent and able to breathe on his own, maybe he could talk. Both he and the nursing staff agreed to try it.

After the plug was in, I leaned over him, with my ear very close to his lips. Word by excruciatingly-sighed word, at a snail's pace, he said,

"I . . . (breath . . .)
am . . . (breath . . .)
a kriyaban. . . . (breath . . .)
I am . . . (breath . . .)
a follower . . . (breath . . .)
of . . . (breath . . .)
Yogananda!"

And a light—needing no sun nor electricity to shine—permeated the room! I saw in him so much wisdom that it seemed to overshadow all that I had entertained him with. I was overwhelmed with joy and could hardly contain myself.

That was all he had strength for, the first time.

What manner of man was this? What did he know? Where had he been?

Daily, he would speak for as long as he could until needing to be suctioned and the ventilator turned on. He carefully chose his words so as not to waste his energy. And when I was away from him, I would meditate on ways to help him say what he wanted to say. Often he spoke leaving out words that just took up strength, nevertheless I could understand what he was saying.

He spoke of his beliefs, and I heard my very own come from his lips with more for me to consider. He had so much he wanted to say. Time was precious, and I felt his frustration when his strength would give out. With laying on of hands, he would become calm.

As if he knew, sadly, our time together was short-lived, for his physical existence was very fragile. Eventually he came down with pneumonia, and unable to fight it, passed over.

His girl friend gave me all of his Buddhist possessions, which he wanted me to have. There were candle holders, statues, a prayer wheel and incense burners. I gave most of it to Song of the Morning and kept two items to remember him by.

Placed in my life are people who carry spiritual energy that sustains me. They are many and are all ages and of all faiths.

* * *

George and I were asked if we would like to go to a bonfire at the retreat. This brought to mind memories of bonfires on the shore of Lake Michigan when I was younger. It was such fun sitting on a blanket with friends, gathered around a fire roasting hot dogs and marshmallows. It seemed we always managed to eat some sand with them. We would talk, laugh and sing our way late into the night. I was looking forward to this now.

When we arrived at the bonfire, I was shocked at the size of it. Within a clearing in the forest, wood and branches were stacked to the size of a small house, and it was all aflame. Fear came forth from me because of the immense size of the fire. I was afraid for man and nature.

I saw the maintenance man throwing gas on the blazing fire, and the flames would come back toward him as if they were hungrily eating up the stream and wanted more. Each time, he would pull back just before he was consumed. Over and over, he did this dance of chance.

It had not rained recently, so I didn't feel such a large fire was safe. This was nothing like the bonfires I knew of on the shoreline of Lake Michigan in my childhood. I was very unsettled and worried for the forest.

I began to circle the bonfire. Walking around its circumference, I could see the danger to the surrounding trees that were not too far from the fire's edge. Sparks were floating everywhere and were being carried by the warming air toward the forest in all directions.

I surrendered to the experience, then found myself calling upon my Pink Angel to help.

Oh . . . great Pink Angel come and see . . .
sparks in the sky threaten the trees.
Make safe the forest from what might be.

Suddenly there, on this starry night,
she embraced the blaze with wings of light.

Then she smiled at me, as if in reply,
while a gentle rain fell from a cloudless sky.

Calmed, I turned to George and said, "We can go home now." Since then the Retreat has never had another "bonfire" like that one.

Chapter Seventeen

Sylvan Love Song

The love of God, unutterable and perfect,
flows into a pure soul the way that light
rushes into a transparent object.

The more love that it finds,
the more it gives itself;
so that, as we grow clear and open,
the more complete the joy of loving is.

And the more souls who resonate together,
the greater the intensity of their love,
for, mirror-like, each soul reflects the others.

—Dante

At home, Amy would first soak her arthritic hands in warm water so she could then painlessly and effortlessly serenade George and me with enchanting classical music on her grand piano while we ate our dinner. The two of us, George and I, would sit to eat in silence, while her music filled us. We ate together, walked together and worshipped together. Thus our hearts became entwined. How could it not be so?

For some time, I had been feeling good about the fact that, for once in my life, I did not need a man in order to be happy. It was a refreshing, wholesome feeling . . . hard to explain. I was content with myself and liked my solitude. I could be me. I loved my career. I loved that I was a healer. I could support myself. I made good decisions on my own. I could come and go as I pleased. I could travel to see distant friends or family and invite them to visit me when I wanted to.

Then along came George, someone who truly listened to my spiritual side and didn't find it inconceivable. Here was someone I was happy to be with and seemed compatible with.

We spent a lot of time together. In my journal I wrote:

Isn't it amazing that:

when one of us wants silence,
we both want silence, and all is silent;

when one of us hears nature's symphony,
nature plays for both of us;

when we need each other,
we are there for each other;

when we read each other's thoughts,
we are melded into one, and individual too.

We both like the little things in life.

When we are parted, we are still together.
We are happy. God is loving us.

After a time, we began to contemplate a future together, married and at Song of the Morning in the, as yet, undeveloped Clear Light Community. We wrote some commitments—expressions of our love—which we thought were reasonable.

Sebastian came to me one night and had some things to say about our commitments.

"In your world, your commitment for the present time is no commitment at all. In the higher realms, where there is only 'present time', commitments are not made.

"Pure love is unconditional, limitless, and timeless. If you are able to proclaim true faithfulness and love, you do not need boundaries or limits. Marriage is a blessing, given with a proclamation of faithfulness and pure love, without limits and boundaries.

"For you, this is happening too fast. Take your time to grow in love. To me, your future and past are now."

Then, as if time were irrelevant . . .

ANNOUNCEMENT

In the flowering month of May,
Two hearts will become one.

On Sunday, the 28th day,
You are welcome to come.

10:00 am, prompt . . .
We know it is early for you . . .

You are invited to view
This Ceremony for two.

Follow the moss-covered path
Deep into the woods, if you please . . .

To the Shrine of Christ . . .
Under a canopy of trees.

I pictured myself wearing a pale yellow dress for the wedding. I went to a mall in Traverse City. As I approached the main entrance, I stopped and affirmed, "I am going to find my perfect wedding dress in this mall." And then I went in.

I searched in every store, spent hours looking. Finding nothing, I was discouraged. On my way out of the mall, I passed a teeny-bopper shop. I had gone right on by it earlier because the skinny window mannequins were wearing the latest teenage styles. Desperate, I thought I would give it a try. I went right to a rack in the store and immediately found the perfect dress—soft, pale yellow, with a lovely, eyelet trim around the neck and the hemline—just as I had pictured it.

However, it was several sizes too small, and it was the only one. Disappointed, I was about to leave, when Sebastian appeared and said,

"This is your dress."

I said, "No, it isn't."

He said, "Yes, it is."

I said, "No, it can't be, it is too small!"

He adamantly returned with, "This is your dress!", at which point a sales person came up to me, as if she had replaced him, and asked if she could help me.

I asked her, "Do you have this dress in a larger size?"

"Yes", she said, and took me to a different rack, and there, before my eyes, was my dress!" Thank you, Sebastian!

Several days later, I had walked into the forest and was resting under overhanging branches of trees. There one of nature's spirits reached toward me to get my attention. He attempted to hand me something. They were exquisite gold earrings, and the sunlight streamed down upon them as he showed them to me. He said I should wear them for the wedding. But I could not connect from this world to his, physically, and when he realized this, he simply told me I needed to wear gold earrings for my wedding. When I asked him why, he said, "The finest of gold threads symbolize the oneness between Mother Earth and the Divine, and two hearts as one."

The next day, I went to the home of someone who wanted a healing session. Before I started, she handed me two 18 karat gold earrings to borrow, filigreed with fine threads of gold in the shape of leaves, to wear for our wedding! The very earrings the nature spirit was trying to hand me!

It was as if the ceremony started in the lodge, where women and nature spirits gathered to help prepare me for marriage. In exchanging happy memories, we laughed as if children. And their happiness ignited ever-more joy within me, and so changed me that I was transformed into someone who would not have a single bad picture taken of her on that day.

Sending everyone on before me, I began to walk slowly, deep into the forest at Song of the Morning, meditating on the ferns carpeting the forest floor, and the birds and the wind in the trees greeting me with song. I took off my shoes to walk barefoot on the magical, emerald green, moss-covered path, under a lacy, spring canopy of forest, as if this too were all a part of the ceremony.

I stopped along the way to read the stanzas of poetry we had tied around the trees on the mile-long path, for guests to enjoy as they preceded me to the shrine.

* * *

Now touch the air softly,
Step gently. One, two . . .
I'll love you til roses
Are robin's-egg blue;
I'll love you til gravel
Is eaten for bread,
And lemons are orange,
And lavender's red.

* * *

Now touch the air softly,
Swing gently the broom.
I'll love you til windows
Are all of a room;
And the table is laid,
And the table is bare,
And the ceiling reposes
On bottomless air.

* * *

I'll love you til Heaven
Rips the stars from his coat,
And the moon rows away in
A glass-bottomed boat;
And Orion steps down
Like a diver below,
And Earth is ablaze,
And Ocean aglow.

* * *

So touch the air softly,
And swing the broom high.
We will dust the grey mountains,
And sweep the blue sky;
And I'll love you as long
As the furrow the plough,
As However is Ever,
And Ever is Now.

—William Jay Smith[44]

Those who had gathered at the Christ Shrine for the wedding were presented with a choice of semiprecious stones from a bowl. They were instructed to hold the stone during the ceremony and fill it with love and good intentions for our marriage.

And there, at the Christ Shrine, with Jesus' picture alive with light, George was waiting for me, in a light all his own, for us to be married. There was no mistaking his happiness nor mine. And the world shed pure delight on our love. The sun was bright and the sky was blue, the forest greener than ever and the ferns abundant, and the birds sang. And Jesus, Sebastian and nature spirits were there.

Here, within this lovely, living, emerald cathedral, a guitarist played music and sang with the birds and forest dwellers. In a ceremony, using our words and the words of others, we were married by a dear friend, in the company of family, friends, and others who just happened by, and those unseen.

God showered blessings on us that day, as we placed rose garlands over each other, listened to poetry and readings we had selected, spoke vows of love, exchanged rings, and sealed our marriage with a kiss. All in a wink of an eye.

When the ceremony ended, the minister handed us a lovely, frosted, rose-colored bowl, and, as people lined up to wish us well, they each put their love-filled, semi-precious stone into our beautiful bowl. We cherish these symbols of love and affection. They remind us of our marriage and the love we have for each other, when we perchance look upon them.

Ever sharing with Jesus . . . "Ah, Sweet Jesus, how quickly the ceremony ended, and yet how long it remains in memory. The setting could not have been more beautiful than this—God's—cathedral."

We attended the Sunday morning service after the wedding, and during a meditative time while I was sitting on the floor, the guitarist came over, sat down near me, and started to accompany me while I sang "Evergreen"[45] to George.

Friends made a special Sunday dinner at the Retreat, with a wedding cake, bon-bons, and toasts. Our friend Victor read a poem he had written for us. It was truly a blessed, beautiful spring day, full of enchantment, in the year two thousand.

Shortly after we were married, George was rototilling the vegetable garden at the Retreat and found a beautiful, polished stone. When he looked closely at it, its translucent, intricate patterns of milky white, indigo and shades of brown drew him deep into it. It had a cosmic significance for him and represented the heavens above and the earth below, in their infinite magnificence and mystery. And between the two, a membrane covers the earth, as if demarking a layer in the atmosphere. Just below a bulge in the membrane, a translucent capsule shaped like an egg, sits upon the earth. He showed it to me, and as I gazed at it, I saw all that he saw.

It was truly a gift nature meant for him to find just as the earrings were meant for me. He placed it in the bowl with the other stones from our wedding.

And I heard Sebastian say,

"So, God of marriage,
we've brought them this far;
the rest of the song
is their singing."

Ah, My Dear Husband,

What joys you have given me.
Your closeness and tenderness
give me comfort when I need it.
Your touch is healing
to my heart and soul.
Your voice is that of angels.
Your humble wisdom directs me to
new keys of my being,
gives me thoughts to ponder and wonder
in deeper understanding.
Your kindnesses fill me.
My cup overflows.
I pray that I can give
as you have given,
and love as you love.

Ah, Dear Wife

You are the jewel of my life,
the precious treasure I have found.
You radiate enthusiasm every day,
and as you scatter love light all around,
the chains that bind drop to the ground.
For how can thought of limitation,
lack, or fear survive the power of light?
When mind is purposeful
and guided by what's right,
then unseen forces join to help us in our work.
They shape our thinking, amplify our might.
Dear Heart, I love you
for the goodness of your soul.
Your perseverance, bold initiative, and fire
bring both of us much closer to our goal,
as each of us supplies what both of us require
God's work to do and others to inspire.

Chapter Eighteen

Think of God

LIFE'S PROCESS

The lily blossom did not just appear.
The lily had to grow—
from bulb beneath the ground
to stem and leaves—
then bud and blossom in the light and air,
to waft its sweet perfume
and show its vibrant colors fair.

And when the beauty of the lily fades
and petals fall,
its life retires into the bulb and waits
until its season for rebirth again does call.

So too, our spirit on this earth
does blossom and bring forth
the beauty latent in it from our birth,
as we progress in love and wisdom, joy and mirth.

—George Johnston

Ah . . . dear forest spirit, whatever or whomever you sustain within your heights and depths, we honor you and apologize for whatever harm we might do you in our endeavor to live amidst all you hold dear.

We who so anxiously want to live under your canopies, experience your changing seasons, smell your fragrant pine and flower, play among the ferns, and discover your nature spirits within their hiding places . . . above all, we want to do no harm.

Our one-acre, wooded lot, four hundred feet from the river, is part of eight hundred acres of privately-owned land adjoining the Pigeon River State Forest.

Two spruce trees stand tall, towering above the others, as if a majestic portal, and we consider centering our new home between them. Ours will be the first home in the new Clear Light Community at Song of the Morning Retreat.

As we walked on the lot, we realized it had been walked upon in ages past but never disturbed, nor did it hold within its bounds spirits of failure. I felt a strong presence guarding it.

We researched what type of house we would build a year before we actually built it. At first, we thought we might like a dome, so we visited a completed dome home. Next, we thought we would build a two-story chalet, then a log home. It was a difficult process. And then . . .

I saw, in vision clear.
They showed me what could be:
a forest dwelling, low and fair,
that blended with the trees.

We studied the lay of the land, colors of the forest, direction of the house, and feng shui principles, and had a clear picture of how our final choice—a simple, one-story home—would feel and blend in with the land and trees.

Since we were the first to build in the Clear Light Community, it was a lengthy process. Many permits had to be sought. The roads were just in and bringing in power took more time. The best cell phone available for our isolated area was a bag phone and only worked part of the time, but it was our only means of outside communication for over a year, until land lines were installed to our house. Our mailbox was a mile away. All was perfect, even in its imperfections.

Throughout the building process, I would contemplate the reasoning behind such a slow, challenging, pioneering task and why we would even undertake it. An inner voice or prompting had initially advised me to "Sell, buy and move in," as if to say it would be easier on us to buy something already built. Jesus neither encouraged nor discouraged me. Sebastian said, "You will set an example," and when I would look at Yogananda's picture, he seemed pleased and appeared to be winking at me, as if we were an important part of something that he wanted. George simply felt that building in the community was what we were supposed to do and never gave it a second thought.

I cannot begin to tell you how wonderful it is to be living here, in the quiet of the Retreat, amidst God's creations. Every window gives us ever-changing views as the sun creeps across the sky, transforming the moods of nature with variations of light and darkness. It's as if nature ornaments our home, our lives.

Every day, I greet the morning here in the forest . . . a taste of life different from ordinary ways, for a genuine, undemanding spirituality is abundant here. I step outside with a cheery "Good morning" directed at the many expressions of beauty and life that surround us.

As I rest in Him with absolute, steadfast faith,
heaven's gifts spread out before me
in earth tones sweet and inviting.

The flowers in our gardens are vibrant, unblemished ferns cover the forest floor, and the birds sing morning greetings. I am drawn to new growth, fadings away, and the tracks of those who visited during the night.

The congregations of trees bend and creak in the wind and have their own fragrances. I often single out individual ones with which to share certain joys or release periodic bits of depression or frustration, as each tree imparts its own unique qualities.

When I stand outside, looking at our home from a distance, I recognize it as the same one I saw in the vision.

I love silence; so does George. But there is more silent

listening than silence. You might think it would be very quiet here, and by some standards it surely is. However, the wind, rustling leaves, wind chimes, raindrops on the roof, humming-bird wings, the buzz of bumblebees, woodpeckers pecking, Canandian geese honking, a myriad of bird songs, and the chatterings of racoons, chipmunks and squirrels, all—in heavenly, orchestrated timing—fill the air with harmonious sounds and rhythms.

I have always been a wanderer, non-attached to a building, place or situation, and here I am settling in, as if forever.

Summer turns gently into a glorious autumn, then into the white of winter. And in the dark, wee hours of morning, I set the thermostat higher and build a fire in the wood stove. If I were better able to withstand the cold, I wouldn't bother with the furnace. It takes a bit of time for the fire in the stove to get things warmed up, but when it does the furnace shuts off.

In the early morning hours, I often sit in my rocker, sipping hot tea, looking out our sliding glass doors, in and out of meditation. Even though I am on the inside of the sliders and nature is outside, I am always drawn into the whole of it. So much in nature remains hidden unless you contemplate on it long enough. I watch the shadowy colors of the white, wintry scene gradually change as the sun slowly rises. Snow glistens like diamonds as the sun meets it on the ground, on branches and in the air.

The beautiful view is always uplifting and entertaining.

Deer come into our yard, looking for food. They paw the snow-covered ground to find clover. On rare occasions, an elk strolls through. Turkeys, in whole flocks, come too, pecking for food. Chickadees and blue jays play at the bird feeder, and racoons along with red, brown, black and grey squirrels, try to outsmart us in getting at the bird seed. Also, there are the never-ending antics of the friendly chipmunks.

Our home here at Song of the Morning, within a community of like-minded people, is a perfect setting from which to write. Writing this book has caused me to relive much joy and suffering. It has opened up past memories of abuse that my children and I had kept buried for thirty years. The process of sharing our memories and feelings with each other has helped us heal old emotional wounds, and we have grown closer still.

My small closet office is crowded—books and papers surround me. Yet, even amidst such disorder and the hectic pace of my life, when I sit down to write, words often flow from out of deepest prayer, within a time outside of time. I am of two minds then: one grounded to the sound and presence of my physical self; the other—the mind of my Soul—free as the wind. The presence of Jesus and other masters—or even just the thought of them—often fills me with love and inspiration to share . . . sometimes with blissful experiences I keep in silence within my heart.

There are other times when I feel as if I am in a time-out period, when instead of being able to focus on God, my attempts to meditate become entwined with assimilating past spiritual experiences, my concerns as a writer, woes of the world and those close to me, and other matters that draw my attention away from God. Sometimes these periods last for weeks, and during these times, even though I have a constant sense of God's presence, I don't feel drawn to call upon God and the Holy Ones.

I used to wonder why I would allow such spiritual limitation to enter my being and why I couldn't seem to pull myself up from the depths of it. On occasion, the thought would flash through my mind that maybe I had done something to displease God, or I had had my share of ecstasy—as if there was only a limited amount to hand out and I should be grateful and content with what I had received. I didn't yet understand the ebb and flow of all aspects of earthly life, including the spiritual.

Over time, I learned to surrender ever more to God and accept these less-blissful periods of spiritual dormancy and introspection with a grateful heart.

I still have such times-out, but having had them before, I know they are temporary and that, at some moment, I will be taken by surprise with new visions and experiences holding ever-more lessons, with or without having yearned for more, simply by dwelling in love and appreciating life.

If life ever seems to be on hold for you and spiritual or material difficulties come to strengthen you or teach you some important lesson, don't lose faith. Every moment allows one to pray and look within for guidance, to make a fresh start, to persevere.

Think of God, meditate, do God's will every day, and you will cultivate a relationship with your Creator that will sustain and guide you through any storm. Become happier by being kind to all and embracing life with gratitude, knowing that there is a purpose in every trial that comes your way. For a loving, thankful heart, faithful and true, opens doors to heaven and multiplies one's blessings.

Just as a lily grows toward the sun to blossom and bring forth its inherent beauty, truly your soul will shine more brightly as it grows closer and closer to God, finally to become infinite, immaculate light—one with God.

☼

And now our hearts are free

to think on Thee,

and withhold nothing from You,

as if we ever could.

ENDNOTES

CHAPTER THREE: STICKS AND STONES

1. Leo F. Buscaglia, author of *Love: What Life is All About,* Ballantine Books, 1972, wrote five best-seller books and many other inspirational books on the topic of love.

2. Jay G. Silverman, PhD; Anita Raj, PhD; Lorelei A. Mucci, MPH; and Jeanne E. Hathaway, MD, MPH, "Dating Violence Against Adolescent Girls and Associated Substance Use, Unhealthy Weight Control, Sexual Risk Behavior, Pregnancy, and Suicidality," *Journal of the American Medical Association*, Vol. 286, No. 5, 2001.

3. Jesus speaks of free will in *Messages from Jesus – A Dialogue of Love,* Mary Ann Johnston (see its index). *http://www.MessagesfromJesus.com.*

4. Stephany Alexander, *http://www.womansavers.com*

5. "Heart to Heart for battered men and women," *http://www.heart-2-heart.ca/women/page5.html.*

6. The Commonwealth Fund, "Health Concerns across a Woman's Lifespan," 1998 Survey of Women's Health, May 1999.

7. Valerie J. Packota, B.A., B.S.W., M.S.W. h*ttp://www.springtideresources.org/resources/show.cfm?id =44*

8. Pat Davies, Melinda Smith, M.A., Tina de Benedictis, Ph.D., Jaelline Jaffe, Ph.D., and Jeanne Segal, Ph.D., Domestic Violence and Abuse: Signs and Symptoms of Abusive Relationships. *http://www.helpguide.org/mental/domestic_violence_abuse_types_signs_causes_effects.htm.*

9. Carlson, Bonnie E. (1984). "Children's observations of interpersonal violence," Pp. 147-167 A.R. Roberts, 1984.

10. Women's Rural Advocacy Programs. "Why Women Stay, the Barriers to Leaving". *http://.www.letswrap.com/dvinfr/index.htm.*

11. Domestic Violence – Battering Women, Physical abuse. *http://www.allaboutcounseling.com/domestic_violence.htm.*

12. Bob Carver, "Understanding Mental and Emotional or Psychological Abuse," *http://www.cyberparent.com/abuse/mentalemotionalabusers.htm*

13. A. Helton, "Battering during pregnancy," *American Journal of Nursing* , August 1986.

14. The Riley Center, "About Domestic Abuse – Myths," St. Vincent de Paul Society, *http://www.rileycenter.org/index.html.* 15, Galatians 3:28

16. Knowledge Universe, *http://www.pcsdma.org/Knowledge%20Universe.htm.*

17. Why Battered Women Stay With Their Batterers. *http://www.co.lake.il.us/statesattorney/violence/whywomenstay.asp*

18. Joseph S. Volpe, Ph.D., B.C.E.T .S. "Effects of Domestic Violence on Children and Adolescents: An Overview," The American Academy of Experts in Traumatic Stress, Inc. 1996, *http://www.aaets.org/article8.htm*

19. "Stat" in medical language is actually not an acronym; it's short for "statim", the Latin word for immediately.

CHAPTER FOUR: GRASS IN WINTER

20. Steven Stosny, "Why marriage counseling has failed," *http://compassionpower.com/index.php.*

21. Turning Point. *http://www.turningpoint6.com/pages/faq.shtml.*

22. Albert R. Roberts, *"Crisis Intervention Handbook: Assessment, Treatment and Research, Third Edition,"* Oxford University Press, USA 3rd edition, 2005. ISBN-13: 978-0195179910.

23. Several years later, Mary Ann helped raise funds to implement Choices in her hometown.

24. *http://www.helpguide.org.*

25. Gisela Fosado. Article: "Women, Prisons and Change," *http://www.barnard.edu/sfonline/prison/intro_01.htm*

26. Biderman's Chart of Coercion, "The process of abusive brainwashing," *http://www.heart-2-heart.ca/men/page3.html*

27. U.S. statistics through *http://www.aadainc.org/Statistics.htm.*

28. Buddy T., BS psychology, "Domestic Abuse – Why Do They Do It", *http://www.alcoholism.about.com/cs/abuse/a/990407.htm*

29. "Firearms and Intimate Partner Violence," Johns Hopkins University Center for Gun Policy and Research, 2003, *http://www.jhsph.edu/gunpolicy/IPV_firearms.pdf*

30. "A Deadly Myth: Women, Handguns, and Self-Defense." Violence Policy Center. Washington, DC., *http://www.vpc.org/studies/myth.htm* 2001.

CHAPTER SEVEN: NEW HORIZONS

31 Sue Monk Kidd, author of *The Dance of the Dissident Daughter,* began to question her role as a woman in her culture, family, and church, and writes of her journey from Christian tradition to a more enlightened perspective.

32. Henrik Ibsen, *A Doll's House*, translated by William Archer, ©John W. Lovell Co., 1890, pp. 119-120.

33. Saint Teresa of Avila, *The Life of Saint Teresa of Avila*, Penguin Books, 1958.

34. I Corinthians 12: 4-11

35. Ethan Walker, in *The Mystic Christ*, p. 235, writes of the ego's subversive, self-serving nature giving us a sense of separation from God.

36. Jesus speaks of the ego in *Messages from Jesus -A Dialogue of Love,* Mary Ann Johnston, Tatienne Publishing. (see its index) *http://www.MessagesfromJesus.com.*

37. Dr. Barbara Brennan, author of *Hands of Light* and *Light Emerging*, founded Healing Touch™, a hands-on, intuitive healing system that includes becoming aware of and correcting deep-seated, negative thought patterns in a person's mind, as well as distortions in their energy field, in order to improve physical, emotional, mental, and spiritual health and well-being.

38. Gregg Braden writes of non-attachment to outcome in his book, *The Divine Matrix*.

CHAPTER EIGHT: AN AWAKENING

39. The dormant kundalini energy at the base of the spine, when aroused, travels upward and opens centers of spiritual awareness (chakras) in the astral spine and brain. As a result, one awakens to perceptions and intuitions on dimensions beyond the physical. Normally, a kundalini awakening is gradual, but it can be sudden and can affect the physical body.

40. Song of the Morning is a yoga retreat in Vanderbilt, Michigan. *http://www.goldenlotus.org*.

CHAPTER THIRTEEN: LET YOUR RELIGION BE LOVE

41. James 1:27

42. Throughout Carol Riddell's book, *The Findhorn Community,* she writes of spiritual gardening, using meditation techniques as an integral part of the practice. The Findhorn Press, 1991.

CHAPTER FOURTEEN: YOGANANDA

43. Paramahansa Yogananda, *Autobiography of a Yogi*, Self-Realization Fellowship Publishers, 2006.

CHAPTER SEVENTEEN: SYLVAN LOVE SONG

44. A Pavanne for the Nursery, Smith, William Jay. *The world below the Window*: Poems 1937-1997. pp. 103. ©1998 William Jay Smith. Reprinted with permission of The Johns Hopkins University Press.

45. p. 191. From the motion picture, *A Star is Born*.

INDEX

BOOKS FOR THE HEART AND MIND

——*A Course in Miracles,* © Foundation for Inner Peace, Viking Penguin, 1996.

——*Blessed Souls, Teachings of Karunamayi,* Sri Matrudevi Visvashanti Ashram Trust, 1998.

——*Gospel of Thomas: Annotated & Explained,* Translator: Stevan L. Davies, Skylight Paths Publishing, 2002.

Amritaswarupananda, Swami
Ammachi, A Biography of Mata Amritanandamayi, Mata Amritanandamayi Center, 1994.

Braden, Gregg,
Awakening to Zero Point, LL Productions, 1996.
The Isaiah Effect, Harmony Books, 2000.
The Divine Matrix, Hay House, 2006.

Brennan, Barbara
Hands of Light: A Guide to Healing Through the Human Energy Field, Bantam Books, 1987.
Light Emerging, Bantam Books, 1993.

Buscaglia, Leo F.,
Love: What Life is All About, Ballantine Books, 1972.

Cameron, Julia,
The Artist's Way, J.P.Putnam's Sons, 1992.
Finding Water, The Art of Perseverance, Penguin Group, 2006.

Chopra, Deepak,
The Third Jesus: The Christ We Cannot Ignore.
Harmony, 2008.

Dante, Alighieri (author), John Ciardi (translator)
The Divine Comedy, NAL Trade, 2003.

Gandhi, Mohandas,
Gandhi an Autobiography, Beacon Press, 1967

Gibran, Kahlil,
Jesus the Son of Man, Alfred A. Knopf, Inc., 1999, ©
1928 by Kahlil Gibran.

Green, Glenda,
Love Without End: Jesus Speaks, Spiritis Publishing,
1998.

Hicks, Esther and Jerry,
The Astonishing Power of Emotions, Hay House, 2007.

Ibsen, Henrik,
A Doll's House, translated by William Archer, John
W. Lovell Co., 1890.

Johnston, George O.
A Course in Yoga, Self Published, 2007. (For
information go to: www.TatiennePublishing.com.)

Johnston, Mary Ann,
Sustained by Faith – Personal Awakening in God,
Tatienne Publishing, 2008.
http://www.SustainedbyFaith.com

Johnston, Mary Ann,
Messages from Jesus - A Dialogue of Love, Tatienne
Publishing, 2009.
http://www.MessagesFromJesus.com

Kidd, Sue Monk,
The Dance of the Dissident Daughter, HarperOne,
2006.

Lakshmi Devi, Sai Maa,
Petals of Grace, Essential Teaching for Self Mastery,
HIU Press, 2005.

Lao Tsu,
Tao Te Ching, Vintage Books, 1989

Lasko, Leonard,
Healing With Love, Harper Collins, 1992.

Levi,
The Aquarian Gospel of Jesus the Christ, DeVorss
Publications, 2003. Original copyright 1907.

Markides, Kriacos C.,
Homage to the Sun, Penguin Group, 1987.
*Magus of Strovolos: The Extraordinary World of a
Spiritual healer,* Penguin Group, 1989.
Riding With the Lion, Penguin Group, 1995.
Fire in the Heart, Penguin Group, 1996.

Merzel, Dennis Genpo,
Big Mind – Big Heart: Finding Your Way. Big Mind
Publishing, 2007.

Moore, Thomas,
The Re-enchantment of Everyday Life, Harper
Perennial, 1997.

Morgan, Marlo,
Mutant Message Down Under, Harper Collins
Publishers, 1994.

Myss, Caroline,
Anatomy of the Spirit, Three Rivers Press, 1996.

Entering the Castle: An Inner Path to God and Your Soul, Free Press, 2007.

Ram Dass,
Still Here: Embracing Aging, Changing, and Dying, Riverhead Trade, 2000.

Redfield, James,
The Celestine Prophecy, Warner Books, 1997.

Riddell, Carol,
The Findhorn Community, The Findhorn Press, 1991.

Saint Teresa,
The Life of Saint Teresa, translated by J.M. Cohen, Penguin Books, 1958.

Schulz, Mona Lisa,
Awakening Intuition, Using Your Mind-Body Network for Insight and Healing, Harmony Books, 1998

Stearn, Jess,
A Prophet in His Own Country: The Story of Young Edgar Cayce, William Morrow and Company, Inc., 1974.

Sutherland, Patricia
Perilous Journey: A Mother's International Quest to Rescue Her Children, New Horizon Press, 2002.

Tolle, Eckhart,
The Power of Now: A Guide to Spiritual Enlightenment, New World Library, 2004.

Walker III, Ethan,
The Mystic Christ, Devi Press, 2003.

Warren, Rick,
Purpose Driven Life: What on Earth Am I Here For?, Zondervan Publishing Company, 2007.

White Eagle,
Spiritual Unfoldment Boxed Set, 1960
The Quiet Mind, 1998
The White Eagle Publishing Trust.

Williamson, Marianne,
Everyday Grace, Riverhead Trade, 2004

Young, Sarah,
Jesus Calling: Enjoying Peace in His Presence,
Integrity Publishers, 2004

Yogananda, Paramahansa,
Autobiography of a Yogi, 1994, revised in 1951 by the
author;
Whispers from Eternity; Ninth Edition, 1986;
The Second Coming of Christ, 2004;
*The Yoga of Jesus: Understanding the Hidden
Teachings of the Gospels,* 2007,
Self-Realization Fellowship Publishers

Zukav, Gary
The Seat of the Soul, Simon & Schuster, *1989.*

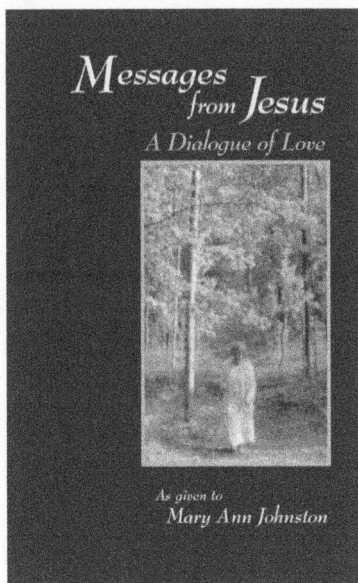

WATCH FOR THE
NEW COVER IN 2009

"Imagine listening to an interview of Jesus of Nazareth. Most of us would be sitting there just praying that the host would delve into the issues that are near and dear to us. In her book, *Messages from Jesus – A Dialogue of Love*, Mary Ann Johnston shares with the world hours of conversation she had with the One known as The Christ. Chances are, if you have a question for Him, the answer lies in these pages, as the essence of the spiritual life, modern religion, world affairs, and disasters are all dealt with rather comprehensively.

"I encourage you to delve into this work and find out for yourself if Truth is present here. My guess is, regardless of what you determine, you won't skip a page."

—Fred Stella,
President, Interfaith Dialogue Association
and Host of Common Threads: An Interfaith Dialogue,
heard weekly on WGVU Radio, Grand Rapids, Michigan

ABOUT THE AUTHOR

Mary Ann Johnston—lecturer, healer, occupational therapist, and author of *Messages from Jesus - A Dialogue of Love* and *Sustained by Faith – Personal Awakening in God*, writes of her spiritual life and conversations with Jesus, who came to her as a radiant ethereal being when she was five years old.

Jesus remained her childhood companion and sustained her throughout seventeen years of an abusive first marriage. Then, several years later, while working as a traveling occupational therapist in rehabilitation facilities across the country, Mary Ann learned—with Jesus' intervention—how to heal people through the power of Spirit.

In 1998, Mary Ann had a spiritual awakening, which increased her creativity and awareness of God's graces. She began to write poetry describing the blissful feelings, visions and realizations she was having. In 2002, Jesus encouraged her to write books, sharing her experiences and his messages of truth and love, with all people, everywhere.

Mary Ann has a degree in occupational therapy from Western Michigan University. She gives homilies and workshops on spiritual subjects addressed in her books, for churches across the country, community groups, and at Song of the Morning yoga retreat in Michigan, where she lives with her husband, George. She is also a talented musician.

Mary Ann is currently writing a third book with Jesus and Yogananda. To read more about her and her husband, or to place an order, go to: http://www.SustainedByFaith.com.

www.ingramcontent.com/pod-product-compliance
Lightning Source LLC
Chambersburg PA
CBHW022014090426
42739CB00006BA/130

9 780981 702742